AMERIC

CRIME

CRIME

by Marianne LeVert

Gerald Leinwand, Ph.D., General Editor

Produced by the Philip Lief Group, Inc.

ιcts On File

GS COMPANY

American Issues: Crime (American Issues Series)

Copyright © 1991 by Gerald Leinwand and The Philip Lief Group

Facts On File, Inc.
460 Park Avenue South
New York NY 10016

Library of Congress Cataloging-in-Publication Data

LeVert, Marianne.
  Crime / by Marianne LeVert; produced by the Philip Lief Group, Inc.
    p.   cm.—(American issues)
  Includes bibliographical references and index.
  Summary: Adresses issues and questions relating to crime in the most violent and crime-ridden country in the industrialized world, the United States.
  ISBN 0-8160-2102-3
  1. Crime—Juvenile literature—United States. [1. Crime.] I. Title. II. Series: American issues (New York, N.Y.)
  HV6789.L47   1991
  364.973—dc20

Facts On File books are available at special discounts when purchased in bulk quantities for businesses, associations, institutions or sales promotions. Please contact the Special Sales Department of our New York office at 212/683-2244 or 800/322-8755.

Jacket design by Catherine Hyman
Printed in the United States of America

MP FOF 10 9 8 7 6 5 4 3 2

This book is printed on acid-free paper.

C O N T E N T S

CRIME

Crime and Society

ONE CRIME INDEX OFFENSE EVERY 2 SECONDS
ONE VIOLENT CRIME EVERY 20 SECONDS
ONE PROPERTY CRIME EVERY 3 SECONDS
ONE MURDER EVERY 25 MINUTES
ONE FORCIBLE RAPE EVERY 6 MINUTES
ONE ROBBERY EVERY MINUTE
ONE AGGRAVATED ASSAULT EVERY 35 SECONDS
ONE BURGLARY EVERY 10 SECONDS
ONE LARCENY THEFT EVERY 4 SECONDS
ONE MOTOR VEHICLE THEFT EVERY 22 SECONDS.

These are the Federal Bureau of Investigation's statistics concerning the frequency of various crimes committed in America today. These staggering figures have earned the United States the dubious distinction of being the most violent and crime-ridden country in the industrialized world.

Why is the level of violence so much higher here than in France or Germany, for instance? Are we so very different from other cultures? How do we define the concept of crime and has this concept changed during our history? Is there a uniquely American idea of crime and justice?

Webster's Dictionary defines crime as "an act that violates the law" and makes an interesting distinction between vice, crime, and sin. "Crime," defines *Webster's*, is a "violation of human laws; vice is a violation of the moral law; and sin is a violation of the divine law." While the dictionary makes clear distinctions between these concepts, societies often must struggle to decide what behaviors—which may include what others define as vice and sin—are considered criminal.

Every society in the world, primitive and modern, has some kind of a code of law that reflects its values, norms, customs, and beliefs. Many anthropologists see the need for law and order as basic to all societies. In many ways, crime is culturally subjective; in other words, what constitutes criminal activity in one group may be perfectly acceptable behavior in another. So then who decides? Marvin E. Wolfgang, professor of sociology and law at the University of Pennsylvania in 1978, defined crime as "an act deemed socially harmful by the group which has power to enforce its beliefs" as well as "an act which offends strong, collective moral sentiment."[1]

In a democracy, these two definitions should not contradict one another. In the United States, an ethnically, racially, and religiously diverse democracy, the group which has the power to enforce its beliefs—the government and its law enforcement agencies—is elected by the majority of the people in society who vote. The laws this body creates should reflect the collective sentiments of the majority. In a dictatorship, the laws may reflect the sentiments of only the few who rule.

This country's code of criminal law originated with the body of English common law that the first settlers brought with them to this country. Common law, originally based on an ancient code of unwritten laws, was established by English jurists and then affirmed by the Parliament, which wrote legislation to enforce these laws. Those who wrote the laws for the American colonies adopted in large part the traditions of English common law. Although they would later surrender some of their sovereign authority to the federal government when the U.S. Constitution was written, the colonies and later the states maintained control over their own criminal codes. As will be discussed later, there remain differences in criminal codes between states.

Crimes of Yesteryear

If the definition of crime depends upon the society that makes laws for its people, how do the crimes of yesterday compare to those of modern America? As our society has grown and developed, our definition of crime has also changed. An interesting example of how such evolution occurs is the rise and fall of the Puritan community that founded the Massachusetts Bay Colony in the 1600s.

John Winthrop and his Puritan followers first arrived in Massachusetts Bay in 1630. They came to America after breaking with the Anglican Church of England with the belief that they were chosen by God to "form a covenant amongst themselves to purify the corrupt practices but not the divine nature" of their homeland church.[2] In this society, the church created laws, monitored its citizens' behavior, and meted out punishment.

The Puritans' approach to crime and punishment reflected their view of man and God; society was designed to fulfill the will of God. The community was small and homogeneous, what is called a self-policing society. Rigid social controls existed; for the most part community pressure regulated behavior. Crime and sin were synonymous in this community; a crime against God was a crime against society and a crime against society a crime against God. Crimes of theft, "pickpocketing," and burglary were minor problems in the community. In fact, there were relatively few crimes against people or property.

In this society, laws were written not so much to protect society against the crimes we know today, but rather to define the boundaries of acceptable moral and public behavior. Though the group brought to the colonies English common law heritage, the Puritans began the process of establishing a justice system by writing their own criminal code. That code differed from England's in several ways. For example, the Puritan's 1648 Book of General Lawes and Lybertyes had many more biblical references than either English law or other American colonies' law codes. Indeed, the Old Testament was deeply embedded in the Puritan code of law. For example, an offense might be written in the following manner: "If any man or woman be a witch . . . they will be put to death. Exod. 22 18 Lev."3

Not only were laws deeply religious in nature in this colony, but the society itself was homogeneous—its citizens all had come from the same traditions and backgrounds. If the members of this community were basically in agreement with the general principles and rules of behavior and morality, why would there be any crime at all? Emile Durkheim, a prominent late 19th-century French sociologist, stated that crime is normal, not pathological or abnormal, and is found in all human societies. Even in a utopian community, there would be crime.[4]

Because record-keeping was poor during this period of history, it is difficult to measure accurately the amount of crime being committed, but historians cite drunkenness, challenges to authority (public criticisms of the government, church, or king), fornication, and adultery as some of the more common offenses of the period. The most serious crimes were blasphemy and witchcraft. In fact, rebellion of any sort, including anti-social behavior (as defined by the church) and irreverent talk, were forbidden.

Although fanatical in their religious fervor and tyrannical in their religious intolerance, the Puritan code of punishment was actually somewhat more lenient than that found in England during the same period. By the end of the 1600s, in fact, there were more than 200 crimes that were punishable by death in England; in the Massachusetts Bay Colony, by contrast, there were only about 11 capital offenses. These included murder, rape, adultery, kidnapping, and blasphemy.

Punishment was swift, often brutal, and public. Lesser crimes, like public drunkenness or cursing the governor, were punished by branding and mutilation, whipping, and banishment. Here, as in many societies, not all criminals were treated equally. Material success was equated with dedication to the community, and by 1648 propertied gentlemen were made exempt from whippings. Monetary fines were more common punishment for the upper-class criminal.[5]

These rather barbaric methods of punishment—later to be defined as "cruel and unusual" and considered unconstitutional under the Eighth Amendment—reflected the Puritans' view that man was essentially depraved, cursed by original sin. Since the Puritans believed there was no hope of rehabilitation, public humiliation was used to identify the deviants to the community and to punish them, not to reform them. Their fate was in God's hands. When all else failed, banishment from the community was the most common method of ridding society of its undesirables.

Until the mid-1600s, the laws and the crimes prosecuted in the Massachusetts Bay Colony reflected the values and norms of Puritan society. The colonies began to expand rapidly, however, and immigrants arrived from other countries, bringing with them their own religious and cultural backgrounds. As a result, the Puritans' once firm hold on social and moral order began to slip away.

The newly diverse population, the changing economic structure, and the new towns established by outside traders threatened both the religious and economic nature of the once homogeneous Puritan community. The Salem witchcraft trials and the persecution of the Quakers are seen by some historians as unsuccessful attempts by the Puritans to retain power in a rapidly changing society.

By the 1670s, Boston was overflowing with frontier adventurers, pirates, English convicts sent to the colonies, and servants who had promised seven years' servitude in exchange for passage to America. These settlers came to America in search of land and wages, not the purity of a strict, religious community. With a marked criminal element living in its growing urban center, the colony experienced increases in the kinds of crimes more familiar to us now: burglary, trafficking in stolen goods, and prostitution.

By the time of the American Revolution, the religious influence of the Puritans had declined and the colonies had a more secular outlook in terms of its criminal codes. In a very short period of time, the laws and crimes in America changed dramatically from infractions of religious codes to the wide-ranging crimes of frontier America. Crimes against God were no longer prosecuted; courts had to make time for the increasing numbers of crimes against property and person. The laws changed, in part, because public sentiment changed. The values of the Puritans were not the same as the new population; the definition of crime therefore changed.

For the next two centuries, crime as we define it today began to flourish due to many complex, interconnected factors: immigration, urbanization, establishment of an entrenched lower class, industrialization, and westward expansion, to name a few. In the early 20th century, our nation experienced several new waves of immigration, further stratification of classes, and the rise of organized crime.

Defining Crime Today

There are many ways our criminal justice system classifies modern crime. One distinction our legal system makes is through the use of the terms *mala in se* ("wrong in themselves") and *mala prohibita* ("wrong because prohibited"). Although we can see from our early history that a community's social norms and values strongly influence what laws are enacted and for which crimes nonconformists are punished, certain offenses are seen as serious crimes by almost every society. Even if the line between criminal and noncriminal shifts according to public opinion, some offenses such as murder, rape, and theft, which are present in every society, universally are viewed as criminal.[6] The legal term for these most serious crimes is *mala in se*, offenses seen as inherently evil.

Mala prohibita refers to those offenses which are criminal because some societies have chosen to regulate them. These include drug abuse, prostitution, gambling, and homosexuality, among others. While the Puritans most strongly equated sin and crime, changes in public opinion have resulted in a change in status of certain criminal activities.

In just the last few decades, for instance, our ideas about criminal behavior as well as the ways in which crimes are prosecuted have been dramatically altered. Decriminalizing abortion and adult pornography (as opposed to obscenity, which remains subject to criminal sanctions) are two modern examples of how radical shifts in public opinion can affect the degree to which a certain behavior is viewed as criminal. Another example is possession of the narcotic heroin. In England, heroin addicts may register with clinics or physicians, and the drug is then available to them through prescription; therefore, heroin possession is not a crime for registered addicts. In the United States, however, it is a felony, the most serious offense for all users.

The basic legal distinction our criminal justice system makes between crimes is the classification of felonies and misdemeanors. A felony is a serious criminal offense punishable by death or imprisonment in a state or federal prison. In the United States, murder, armed robbery, and kidnapping are examples of felonies. A misdemeanor is a less serious act that carries a punishment of a fine or imprisonment for less than one year. Public drunkenness, loitering, or disorderly conduct are examples of misdemeanors.

Another classification of crime, established by the Federal Bureau of Investigation (FBI), distinguishes between violent crimes, such as murder, rape, robbery, aggravated assault, and property crimes, which include burglary, larceny-theft, motor vehicle theft, and arson. These two classifications refer to crimes against the person and crimes against property.

There are many types of criminal behavior that are organized according to the group (government, business, corporation, syndicate) to which the offender belongs. White-collar crime is a term first used by Edwin H. Sutherland in 1940 to describe violations of criminal law by people of upper economic status committed during the course of their occupation. While these crimes were long considered less serious than others, recent studies have shown that the amount of money lost through white-collar crime exceeds that of any other crime. In the last few years, cases against stock market executive Michael Milken and the brokerage house Drexel Burnam Lambert have brought white-collar crime to the front pages of international news. Tax evasion, price fixing, embezzlement, swindling, computer tampering, consumer fraud, and inside-trading scams are but a few of the crimes committed by professionals in the hope of personal, professional, or political gain.

Organized crime is defined as criminal activity by a group of individuals, usually bound by ethnic ties, who create and maintain a crime syndicate based on a corporate business structure—with executives, salaries and promotions, and a highly organized political structure. American crime syndicates, which first flourished here during the 19th century, continue to operate at all levels of society, from ownership of nightclubs and gambling casinos to the maintenance of the underground economy of the inner cities—gambling, loansharking, drug trafficking, and prostitution. Extortion, corruption of government and police officials, and murder are but a few of the methods used to maintain power and carry on organized crime activities.

Since the 1920s, when Prohibition gave rise to the organization of a national crime syndicate, organized crime groups have continued to broaden their investments through the enormous capital they have amassed and the national contacts they maintain. Though deeply entrenched and sometimes protected in many areas of business, labor, and government as well as inner city underground economies, law enforcement agencies are having some success in their investigations and prosecutions of leading organized crime figures. From 1984 to 1986, convictions were obtained in three out of four major organized crime trials in New York.

Violation of safety regulations designed to protect public health is another type of modern crime that leads to thousands of deaths each year. Types of violations include building violations, sanitary codes of restaurants, and fire ordinances. An absentee landlord whose apartments provide inadequate heating or unsafe wiring is just one example of a businessperson who can be found criminally negligent if an accident resulting in injury or death occurs on his or her property.

Corruption occurs in every branch of government. Bribes, payoffs, and conflicts of interest continue to plague our government. Charles Silberman, a renowned criminologist and sociologist, stated, "If street crime threatens the social fabric of American life, governmental crime destroys the political fabric by undermining the trust and belief in the government on which our entire political system is based".[7]

Measuring Crime

Although the American public has become more aware of and impatient with the amount of corruption and fraud in its businesses and institutions, our primary concern appears to remain with crimes that we perceive as threats to our personal safety and property.

Public opinion polls taken in 1989 show that the majority of Americans believe that crime is increasing and are now taking measures to protect themselves and their homes.[8] To some extent, the perception that crime is increasing and that our personal safety is in danger is reinforced by the amount of time the media devotes to the subject of violent crime. Still, a recent poll conducted by *Boston* magazine revealed that over half of those polled believe that crime is more serious than the newspapers and television report.[9] Is there more crime today or are we just hearing more about it? How can we be sure that we are not being influenced by those who might use the issue of law and order for their own purposes, such as politicians and newspaper publishers?

Many professionals, including criminologists, researchers, sociologists, and journalists, look to the FBI for current crime statistics. In the 1920s, the International Association of Chiefs of Police formed the Committee on Uniform Crime Records to develop a system of consistent police statistics. To choose which crimes to include, they first established the various offenses known to law enforcement agencies and then evaluated the various crimes on the basis of their seriousness, frequency and region of occurrence, and likelihood of being reported to police. They developed standardized offense definitions to insure nationwide uniformity in crime reporting. Agencies could therefore submit statistics based on these definitions rather than on the criminal codes of their particular state. Then, in 1930, the Attorney General of the United States designated the Federal Bureau of Investigation (FBI) as the federal agency responsible for collecting, disseminating, and releasing annual reports—based on these definitions—to the nation regarding national crime statistics.

The Uniform Crime Report (UCR) of the FBI, a 355-page document in 1988, is the result of a nationwide effort of about 16,000 city, county, and state law enforcement agencies. Reporting data on crimes organized according to 29 categories of offenses, this report is one of the most complex and fascinating documents of crime in America.

The report creates two crime divisions. Murder, rape, robbery, aggravated assault, burglary, larceny-theft, motor vehicle theft, and arson are known as Part I or Crime Index offenses. Data collection for most Part I offenses is quite extensive; included are statistics regarding total volume of offense by geographical region; percentage increase or decrease from previous years; rate of offense per 100,000 inhabitants; total number of persons arrested for the offense; and the clearance rate (or solution rate) for the crime.

To determine who is committing crime in America today, law enforcement officials also include the age, sex, and race of the offender in their reports to the FBI. For murder cases, data on the age, race, and sex of both the victim and offender, victim/offender relationship, type of weapon used, murder circumstance by relationship (felony type, romantic triangle, argument, etc.) are included as well.

Part II crimes are all other offenses, except traffic violations, not included in Part I. These include: fraud, forgery, embezzlement, vandalism, weapons, prostitution, drug abuse violations, gambling, offenses against family and children, disorderly conduct, curfew and loitering, and driving while under the influence. When newscasters refer to the Crime Index, they are referring to the eight crimes in Part I of the Report; when they speak of the total number of arrests, they include both Part I and Part II offenses.

While the UCR is a useful tool for determining general levels of crime in the nation and aiding in the prediction of present and future trends, it is not a perfectly accurate reporting procedure. First, readers may make erroneous generalizations or assumptions about a geographical area, a race of people, or an economic group on the basis of the statistics of this report.

In addition, because crime statistics can only measure how citizens and police are responding to crime—not how many crimes are actually committed—it may well be impossible to measure accurately the total number of crimes committed. It is estimated that only one-third of all crime is reported to the police.

Seasonal changes in population, temporary economic circumstances, and periodic crackdowns of specific offenses can influence the amount of crime in any time period. And simple human error can lead to false data and interpretation. It is also difficult to assess how an individual police officer's personal bias may affect arrest rates.

The recent proliferation of drug-related and gang-related crime dramatically demonstrates the shortcomings of the UCR, for no one is able to determine from the Report the actual correlation between drugs, gangs and crime in our communities. As a result, the FBI is in the process of implementing a new reporting method called the National Incident-Based Reporting System, which will not be in use until the mid-1990s.

In the meantime, another report, issued twice a year by the United States Department of Justice, helps fill in some of the gaps left by the Uniform Crime Report. The Bureau of Justice Statistics' National Crime Survey includes interviews of more than 100,000 people in about 50,000 households. Through these interviews, the survey is able to extract vital information about both reported and unreported crimes, such as wife or child abuse, as well as in-depth characteristics of offenders as perceived by the victims. Combined with the UCR, this survey presents the most accurate a picture of crime, offenders, and victims available.

Though we will refer to the UCR for current crime statistics in this book, it would be wise to keep in mind some of the criticisms and shortcomings just discussed.

Today's Crisis

Given that there are many problems inherent in determining how much actual crime there is, including the influence of the media, our own fears and prejudices, and the interpretation of crime statistics, there are nevertheless certain facts regarding crime in America on which we can base our discussion.

The Uniform Crime Report for 1988, the latest available, indicates that all eight Part I offenses rose in 1988. For a five-year period (1984 to 1988), violent crime increased 23% and property crime increased 16%. Incidents of homicide rose 1% from 1987 to 1988, claiming a total of 20,675 victims and accounting for 1% of the violent crimes reported.

Although all crime is of great concern to us, it is the physical violence that scares us most. Today, violence has taken over our cities, put battered wives and abused children out of their homes and into hospitals, and made our young people both perpetrators and victims. What do these trends say about our society? How is it that we find ourselves in this crisis? Was there ever a "golden age" of law and order in our country? To help us answer these questions, we will now explore the historical roots of current trends in violence in America.

Notes

1. Marvin Wolfgang, "Real and Perceived Changes in Crime and Punishment," *Daedalus, Journal of the American Academy*

of Arts and Sciences (Winter 1978) pg. 143.

2. Frank Browning, *The American Way of Crime: From Salem to Watergate* (New York: G.P. Putnam's Sons, 1980), pg. 18.

3. Samuel Walker, *Popular Justice: A History of American Criminal Justice* (New York: Oxford University Press, 1980), pg. 12.

4. Wolfgang, pg. 143.

5. Browning, pg. 23.

6. Op. cit., pg. 144.

7. Charles Silberman, *Criminal Justice, Criminal Violence* (New York: Random House, 1978), pg. 46.

8. George Gallop, Jr., *The Gallop Report*, Report Nos. 282–283 (Princeton, N.J., March/April 1987), pg. 7.

9. Susan Steinway, "The Great Scare," *Boston*, February 1990, pg. 111.

CHAPTER TWO

American Violence

While every society has its share of crime and violence, the United States has the highest rate of reported murders, rapes, and robberies among countries that keep crime statistics. We have seven to 10 times the risk of death through homicide than most European countries and Japan claim. Our closest competitor, Finland, has only one-third our homicide rate.[1]

Violence is not, of course, unique to the United States. Throughout history and in every civilization, examples can be found of man's inhumanity and brutality. Millions of people have been tortured and killed in the name of passion, patriotism, and religion: 8,000–10,000 Huguenots in France in 1572, millions of Jews by the Germans during World War II, millions of Soviets at the hands of Stalin, and millions of Cambodians by the Pol Pot regime. The violence in our history, with the exception of the policy of genocide carried out against the Native Americans, has never approached this level. Nevertheless, as we will explore in this chapter, it is this type of violence against religious, ethnic, political groups that characterized our beginnings, rather than isolated incidents against individuals by individuals.

The startling differences in the amount of crime between the United States and other countries may be rooted in our status

15

as a relatively young nation. In just 200 years, we have become one of the richest, most powerful nations in the world. The kind of intense growth and change required to achieve such a position has certainly contributed to the unrest and instability we are now experiencing.

In addition, we have perhaps the most diverse population in the world—more ethnic groups, religions, and nationalities call the United States home than any other country. Such a mixing of cultures and traditions has itself caused a great deal of tension. Mavin Wolfgang stated that a homogeneous culture "promotes a social bond and collectivity, a sense of us being alike and together." In heterogeneous communities, such as the United States, "the pluralism of ethnic groups tend to promote separateness, anonymity, and alienation."[2]

In uncovering the reasons behind our current crisis, we must examine our unique history: How we formed our nation and its values, how we resolved conflict, and how we integrated the many ethnic and religious groups who have come to this country are all important clues as to why the United States is today the most violent nation in the Western world. If we have racial unrest today, what does our history tell us about our treatment of minority groups? If poverty is linked to crime, what can our history tell us about our policies toward those more disadvantaged? What can we learn about guns from our past that might help us understand why we have the highest death rate from firearms?

Our History of Violence

Part of the concern we voice about the level of violence in our country stems from the belief that we are a "civilized" country, one founded on principles of freedom and democracy, and one that strives to provide a fulfilling life for all its citizens. Although the Civil War is our only domestic war, Americans have a long history of domestic turbulence beginning with the very way in which this country was founded. With firearms and force, the European settlers appropriated the land from Native Americans who had lived on this land for centuries.

Another important factor in the development of criminal and racial violence in this country today is that, for the first 100 years of our history, the institution of slavery was a fact of life. The effects of this century-long brutality and inhumanity still reverberate today.

Third, although often called the Great Melting Pot because of the diversity of its population, the United States has not always welcomed immigrants. Indeed, there has been a pattern of violence directed against new ethnic, religious, and political groups by those people who had already settled and prospered here.

The settling of the West in the mid-1800s, the labor struggles at the turn of the century and during the Great Depression, the continued growth and influence of organized crime, and the resistance to the Civil Rights movement in the 1950s and 1960s are all important factors in the history of violence in America. And, no less telling, are the ways in which our society and culture has glorified the very violence that now terrorizes us. All of these influences are important clues to our current crisis.

Conquering America's First Citizens

Although our Thanksgiving holiday has its roots in the early friendship between the Massachusetts Pilgrims and native Indian tribes, the cooperative spirit it commemorates was short-lived. As farmland dwindled, colonists looked for new lands, inevitably leading to invasions of Indian territory. The settlers at first offered goods or money in exchange for property; later they used any and all methods possible to acquire Indian land. The Indians were happy to trade with the European arrivals, but they believed they were granting settlers the right simply to use—not to own—the land. Instead, they were losing their territories forever.

Conflicts arose from the white settlers' misunderstanding of and refusal to learn anything about Indian culture. The Indians' tie to the land had nothing to do with ownership of property; the land and its produce were seen as part of Mother Earth, to be shared and held in common. As Chief Tecumseh of the Shawnees said, "Sell a country? Why not sell the air, the great sea, as well as the earth?"[3]

When efforts to trade peacefully with the Indians failed, the Europeans did not hesitate to take up arms against them. During the Colonial period alone, there were eight recorded wars with the Indians, including the Pequot War in 1637, which resulted in the extermination of the Pequot tribe and cleared the Connecticut Valley for white expansion.

As more and more Europeans arrived to settle in the New World, land in the eastern part of the continent grew scarce and a push to explore and settle the West began. The courage and boldness of this westward drive is overshadowed by the trickery and brutality with which the settlers laid claim to land already occupied by Native American tribes.

After the settlers won their independence from England, the new U.S. government continued the British practice of recognizing tribes as individual sovereign nations with the authority to make and sign treaties. Between 1778 and 1871, almost 400 treaties were signed, but many were broken by the European settlers in the 19th century as their great push westward gained momentum. The treaties were broken by violence, justified by the white settlers by their need for land and property and their belief that the native people were inherently inferior.

What distinguishes the conflicts and wars with the American Indians from what one might consider the unfortunate but necessary brutality of war is the terrible massacres of whole tribes of men, women, and children by the armed militia and army. Many tribes were attacked by surprise and if the braves were absent from the village, the women and children were killed. Sometimes, as happened on November 29, 1864, at Sand Creek in Colorado, the massacre occurred after the white flag of surrender was raised.

In Paxton, Pennsylvania in 1763, one massacre was the result of a ferocious attack on Indians being sheltered in safety by white townspeople. The list of such massacres is long and bloody, ending in 1890 with the massacre of Sioux Indians at Wounded Knee in South Dakota. Three hundred and fifty Indians began the day on December 29, 1890, after their surrender to Colonel James Forsyth. By day's end, only four men and 47 women and children were left alive.

The exact number of Indians who lost their lives as a result of the European invasion is very hard to estimate; the precise Indian population at the time of white settlement is even uncertain. But it seems safe to say that of perhaps 1,000,000 Native Americans who lived in the area of land we now call the United States when the settlers arrived, only 250,000 remained at the turn of the century.[4] While massacres certainly occurred on both sides, the white settlers, with superior firepower and numbers, virtually wiped out in two centuries a whole race of people who had lived on and worshiped this land for thousands of years.

Although restitution in the form of money and land is being made to many tribes today, there is no way to restore the long-term effects of hundreds of broken treaties, the loss of life, and the loss of culture and identity suffered by Native Americans. The European quest for land led to the massacre and disregard of Indians and their culture. It was the Europeans' quest for economic power that led to the widespread practice of slavery in the United States.

Black Americans in Chains

Africans first arrived in the United States colonies in 1619 when 20 slaves were brought, apparently by accident, to Jamestown, Virginia.

Although the practice of slavery could be found in Africa itself, it would be the Europeans in the 15th century who began the commercial slave trade in earnest. For 300 years, the buying and selling of human beings passed from the Portuguese to the Spanish to the Dutch to the French, and finally to the English, who contributed more to the slave trade than any other single group. In fact, it is estimated that the English brought four times the number of slaves in their ships than all of the other nations combined.

Until about 1640, the slaves brought to Virginia had some kind of vague status of indentureship, much like white servants did. After a period of time during which they worked for little or no wages, indentured servants were freed and allowed to own land. But by the 1660s, Virginia had passed a series of laws that formally and legally recognized the institution of slavery and relegated blacks to a permanently inferior status. By the end of the 17th century, slavery was legally recognized in all of the colonies, although the practice did not take hold in New England or the mid-Atlantic regions. Northerners did, however, involve themselves in the financial rewards of the slave trade, reaping huge profits from the sale and enslavement of human beings.

The institution of slavery grew as the financial rewards did. In 1700 there were 20,000 slaves; by the time of Independence in 1776, this figure had grown to about 500,000. Most of the slave population was located along the southeastern coast where tobacco, rice, and cotton were important crops. The invention of the cotton mill in 1793 and the spread throughout the South of the cotton crop further entrenched slavery as a way of life in this region.

Although in 1787 Congress passed the Northwest Ordinance forbidding expansion of slavery into the midwestern territories and in 1808 closed the African slave trade altogether, the South resisted all pressure to end the practice and relied on an illegal slave market and internal slave trading to continue the practice.

The brutality with which African people were taken from their homeland—it is estimated that one-third died on the long march to the ships and another third on the voyage to America—began the history of violence and oppression for African-Americans in this country. What made it possible for one group of people to enslave another? We may understand some of the political and economic rationalizations for the practice, but what about the ethical, moral, or religious implications?

When creating the Constitution of the United States, how could the founding fathers—after fighting for our right to live without tyranny or bondage to another—stipulate that a slave was only worth two-thirds representation, was just two-thirds a person? Though this clause is seen by historians as a concession made to the South in exchange for their loyalty to the union, it nevertheless symbolizes our ability to see a race of people as inferior, not really human. After the Civil War, slavery was abolished, but political and economic equality was still denied to African-Americans.

The violence against blacks that began in slavery continued long after Reconstruction. The South in particular was unwilling to give up the hostile and violent treatment of African-Americans. Though freed through proclamation, blacks continued to be regarded as second-class citizens and for decades many were murdered by burning and lynching. It is estimated that between 1882 and 1927, 4,951 people, mostly blacks, died at the hands of mobs.[5] Furthermore, public hangings and burnings were sometimes preceded by torture. While other immigrant groups were eventually assimilated into the culture, blacks in many parts of the country were barred from mainstream society. The same thinking that had allowed the institution of slavery was used to keep blacks from equal opportunity.

It would not be until the 1960s, when the federal government and the civil rights movement demanded changes in the laws, that progress was made toward equality. In future chapters, we will discuss the long-term psychological, social, and economic effects of slavery on blacks in American life today.

The Wild West

Our culture is steeped in the legends and myths of the Wild West. Our frontier heroes and villains are many times one and the same; criminologists Sykes and Drabek mused that we remember our sheriffs and outlaws with equal pleasure.[6] In fact, many times the differences between them in practice as well as image were not completely apparent—outlaws and sheriffs often switched sides depending on the offer they received. Wyatt Earp, for instance, was appointed sheriff of Dodge City, Kansas because of his reputation as a gunfighter. He was on the run from a horse-theft charge when the citizens awarded him his sheriff's badge.

Many outlaws were able to continue their careers as successful criminals because of the popular stories told about them that were circulated among the incredulous public. Admiration for their daring deeds and romantic images often caused people to forget the terrible crimes they had committed. The bitter feelings that remained after the Civil War gave some, like Frank and Jesse James, a following in the South, because they had fought for the Confederate cause.

At least 21 movies have been made about a seedy, bucktoothed, "cretin" named Billy the Kid. What attracts our attention to a boy who, by many accounts, was known as a cattle thief and pathological liar? Our frontier outlaws are in many ways our country's version of the English knights in shining armor and Robin Hoods, yet in reality very few were the generous, folk heroes we believe them to be. A popular song about Jesse James holds that:

> "Jesse James was a lad who killed many a man
> He robbed the Glensdale train.
> He stole from the rich and he gave to the poor.
> He'd a hand and a heart and a brain."

According to the *Encyclopedia of American Crime*, however, Jesse James never gave one cent to anyone but himself.[7] But the tales, which both law enforcement and the outlaws themselves exaggerated, made it possible for many an outlaw to build a following and thus to escape capture.

Outlaws of all kinds (cattle rustlers, stage and train robbers, common thieves, bank robbers) preyed on unprotected towns. The lack of effective law enforcement and the rise of criminal activity of all kinds threatened the tenuous stability of the new frontier towns. The settlers who survived the long and dangerous journey to their new homeland were determined to protect themselves from further danger. Communities reacted to threats by organizing secret committees, posses, or common mobs both to defend themselves and to rid their community of undesirables.

Impatient with those whom they considered too concerned with the particulars of the law, like a fair trial by jury, mobs often stormed a jail and lynched the criminal themselves. Often, the sheriff encouraged such behavior, standing idle while the crowd proceeded to capture, try, and execute the accused. It wasn't just the ordinary citizen who demanded protection; wealthy cattle ranchers and railroad owners hired professional gunfighters to protect their property. The landowners called them "cattle detectives" and gave them free reign to protect their investments.

Although such vigilante groups could be found in almost every state in the union except Massachusetts, the centers of vigilante movements were Montana, Texas, and California. Many groups were organized by citizens to protect their families from the growing criminal population, but the potential for abusing their power was great. Some groups that organized themselves for public safety used the group for ridding the communities of those they considered undesirables. Forming regulator or vigilance committees, these organizations elected leaders, drafted constitutions, tried, and executed the accused. The potential for using this power to intimidate and persecute others was tremendous and often times realized.

Taking the law into one's own hands through organized groups, though expedient in times of little or ineffectual law enforcement, also led to the formation of such associations as the infamous hate group, the Ku Klux Klan. These hooded night riders were organized after the Civil War in opposition to Reconstruction. Their aim was white supremacy and the separation of the races; their targets were blacks, Jews, radicals, and Catholics; their method was murder and terror.

By the end of the 19th century, more organized law enforcement, as well as the new technology of the telegraph and the telephone, brought an end to the era of outlaws and gunslingers. Other changes in the American landscape, however, caused another type of violence—one that centered on new arrivals on our shores and the growing labor force.

Immigrants and Labor History

Native Americans and African-Americans were not the only groups of people treated with extreme violence by the first white settlers in the New World. Almost every new immigrant group that came to America in search of freedom and opportunity experienced prejudice, often in quite violent ways. Though the Puritans came to this country to escape religious persecution, they in turn persecuted the Quakers, another religious group that had arrived in the Massachusetts Bay Colony by 1650. The Puritans viewed the members of this new group as heretics and quickly banned their literature and instituted whipping and fines as punishments for Quakerism. By 1661, Quakers could be put to death or "stripped naked, whipped, and run out of town."[8]

The Irish and Germans were especially affected by such brutality and discrimination, partially because of their Catholicism, which the Protestant population—the first to arrive in the New World—found intolerable, and in part because of their poor or working-class backgrounds, their traditions and culture, and their political ideas.

The 1800s saw both an increase in immigration and an increase in racial and ethnic violence. There were anti-Chinese riots in Los Angeles, anti-Italian riots in New Orleans, and the New York City Draft Riots in 1863, which resulted in the murder of over 1,200 blacks. In general, poor people, whether new immigrants or not, did not fare well. In the 1870s and 1890s, during periods of economic depression, vagrancy laws were enacted and enforced in order to "control the movement and behavior of the poor and unemployed."[9]

When the Industrial Revolution began in the United States in the mid-1800s, violence and turmoil increased as America fought its way through the turbulent transformation from an agrarian to an urban society. The factories created during the Industrial Revolution drew large numbers of workers to the cities and the mines for work. In the late 1800s and early 1900s, large numbers of Eastern Europeans, some with long histories of socialist ideas in the working class, came to America and the movement towards unionizing began. For 60 years, from 1877 to 1937, workers in most industries strove for better working conditions and wages through the organization of unions.

Though unemployment insurance, the 40-hour work week and laws against child labor are now an accepted part of the American work life, the road to union recognition was a slow and bloody one. In fact, before a court decision in 1842, unionism was considered to be a "criminal conspiracy."[10] The owners of factories and mines regarded these now accepted demands as threats to their profits, and they were able to obtain national and local support for the suppression of workers. The opposition to unions was also a result of strong anti-socialist sentiment in the country, as many leaders of the union movement declared themselves socialists and communists. Organizers were beaten, arrested, and jailed in part for their political beliefs.

The conditions for workers in the early 20th century were very harsh: Laborers toiled long hours for little pay; many worked in unsafe conditions; and child labor laws were rarely enforced. Groups of miners, steel workers, garment workers and others banded together to demand fair wages, hours, safe working conditions, and the right to organize and form unions.

The resistance of the mine and factory owners to these demands and to the organization of unions led to long and bitter strikes, many of which were broken by the owners through intimidation, violence, and murder. While there was certainly violence and destruction on the part of the workers, time after time the owners ordered that unarmed strikers be fired upon, their families harassed, and their leaders beaten or murdered.

Strikes are still called today when demands for wages and improved working conditions are not met by the owners of corporations or factories, but usually without the widespread violence that accompanied the early struggle for workers' rights.

The Rise of Organized Crime

After the turn of the century, there was a huge recorded increase in crime. Before the 1900s, the rate of homicide was approximately one person murdered in every 100,000; by 1910 it was five in 100,000; in 1920 seven in 100,000; and in 1937 9.7 in 100,000.[11] The violence used against the labor movement certainly contributed to the increase, but another factor was the rise of organized crime. While improvements in methods of crime reporting also may have affected statistics, most historians agree that organized crime consistently has increased the amount of crime and violence in the United States, since about 1920.

The President's Commission on Organized Crime defines this group as a "continuing, structured collectivity of persons who utilize criminality, violence, and a willingness to corrupt in order to gain and maintain power and profit."[12] Organized crime began in this country as soon as demand for illegal goods and services became apparent, and in the 1800s demand was high in our growing urban centers. Most cities had a "vice district," where liquor, gambling, and illicit sex were available.

Attempts to wipe out these vices began as opposition by the native population to the habits of the newly arrived working class, particularly to the drinking and gambling habits of the Irish and German immigrants, whose cultures did not consider either Sunday drinking nor gambling criminal activities. The regulation of morals by the English middle class only drove such activities underground, paving the way for more crime. The various criminal operations, however, could not have existed or flourished without the cooperation and participation of government officials at every level from politician to police.

While Irish immigrants were the first group to control the underground economy of gambling and prostitution, by the end of the 19th century, this position shifted to a new immigrant group: Some Italians brought with them long-standing criminal patterns from southern Italy and Sicily. Before the Volstead Act of 1920 (Prohibition), when the manufacture and sale of alcohol became illegal, organized crime was relatively free from violence.[13] Gambling and prostitution were the primary activities of organized crime, and corruption of officials the method, but when the manufacture and sale of alcohol were outlawed, organized crime stepped in and took over this profitable activity. Not only was there a huge population of those who drank, but it seems that this population increased dramatically with the new prohibition.

Just as the Wild West and its outlaws have been romanticized, the exploits of gangsters like Al Capone and Bugsy Siegel have become the subject of books, movies and television programs that feature them as villainous heroes admired for their skill at violence. Al Capone, called Public Enemy Number One by the Chicago Crime Commission, especially captures the imagination of the public. A vicious murderer known for fits of rage, he was also popularly viewed as a devoted family man and loyal friend. His flashy and flamboyant public life, complete with diamond rings, beautiful women, and long limousines, earned him fan mail from all over the country in addition to the loyalty of corrupt Chicago politicians.

When Prohibition ended 14 years after it began, the syndicates, dominated by criminals from southeastern Italy and Sicily, moved further into regional and national prostitution rings and gambling syndicates, and soon became involved in illegal drug trafficking. These activities and a national base of over 23 "families" provided the opportunity for organized crime to amass tremendous power and wealth. The organization's ability to corrupt government, law enforcement, and labor officials has kept that power from ever being completely destroyed. The Italian Mafia, though losing power in the late 1980s, has remained firmly entrenched in several key industries, maintaining control over construction, garment, and waterfront activities in our large cities.

As we will see in Chapter Four, new groups have moved into the lucrative drug trade and its related criminal activities: Jamaican posses and Chinese triads are among the many who control the underground economy of the inner cities. And though assault weapons may have supplanted machine guns, violence is still the method of protecting territory and profits.

Political and Racial Violence

Quite apart from a continually growing criminal element, Americans have also had to deal with the constant undercurrents of racial violence that have plagued our country since its earliest days. Slavery was a fact of life for blacks until the end of the 1800s and this brutality and oppression did not end with the Civil War. Urban unrest in America led to riots in both 1919 and 1943 as economic, social, and educational segregation of minority groups, most particularly blacks, continued. As the rest of the population prospered following World War II, black Americans, who had also fought in the war, still found themselves excluded.

The decade of the 1960s exploded in violence and murder after several decades of relative calm in the United States. Racial unrest and political assassinations rocked the country, causing the government and its people to take a closer look at the underlying roots of violence. During the 1960s, President John F. Kennedy, Senator and presidential candidate Robert F. Kennedy, and civil rights activists Medgar Evers, Malcolm X, and Martin Luther King Jr. were all assassinated. Massive student demonstrations against the unpopular war in Vietnam resulted in police rioting at the 1968 Democratic National Convention in Chicago and at universities across the nation. Small factions of the anti-war movement engaged in bombings of public and college buildings.

Massive demonstrations for civil rights were led by concerned and dedicated black and white leaders and joined by ordinary and extraordinary citizens. Dr. Martin Luther King, Jr., who was assassinated in 1968, led efforts to move the country forward towards social and economic equality through nonviolence and civil disobedience.

There were approximately 11,400 demonstrations recorded in just three months in 1963.[14] Nonviolent efforts by the protestors were most often met with violence and brutality from the police, as demonstrators, particularly in the South, were attacked by police dogs, high power hoses, billy clubs, and tear gas. In 1963, three children were killed when a bomb exploded in a church in Birmingham, Alabama, and in 1964, three civil rights workers were murdered in Mississippi. During this time, the world watched as Governor George Wallace of Alabama defied federal law by blocking the door to the University of Alabama to keep a black student from entering. Throughout the South, federal troops were called to enforce recently passed legislation that forced schools to integrate.

Much of our country's violence in the past was aimed against minority groups, a trend that continues today. But during the 1960s minorities, particularly blacks in the inner cities, began to turn this violence outward during a tumultuous decade. Frustrated at the slow pace of meaningful change, this anger and rage was directed primarily at property, not persons; the deaths that resulted were overwhelmingly of black people and primarily the result of "shoot to kill" policies used by riot police and National Guardsmen to stop the widespread looting of businesses.

Watts, a poor black section of Los Angeles, erupted in 1965 following rumors of police brutality. Burning and looting were widespread. After riot police and the National Guard were called in, 34 people were dead, 1,032 were injured, 4,000 arrested, and millions of dollars worth of damage had been done to the neighborhood.

Over the next several years, city after city went up in flames; in 1967 Newark and Detroit were the hardest hit. President

Johnson's National Advisory Commission on Civil Disorders in 1968 advised that the rage and frustration that caused these riots were primarily the result of the exclusion of minorities from economic progress through segregation and discrimination. These same conditions have been cited as contributing to the widespread rioting that shook Miami, Florida in 1982 and 1989.

Violence Today

Today, we have many legal safeguards that help prevent the large-scale violence and genocide that occurred in the past. The National Labor Relations Act of 1935, for example, gave unions the right to organize and bargain; police protection and court-ordered restraining orders do result in reduction of domestic violence; anti-discrimination laws help protect minorities from racially motivated discrimination and violence; and child abuse and neglect laws are aimed at protecting children from mistreatment.

These safeguards, however, cannot entirely protect individuals or groups from violence and crime. Police estimate that there has been a 30% increase in "hate crimes" in the last year; New York officials put the increase in their city at about 80%.[15] These are incidents of violence against a particular group; homosexuals, blacks, and Jews are often the targets and young people are often the offenders.

The roots of ethnic and racial violence are deeply embedded in our short history. Genocide, enslavement, vigilante justice, and persecution of many immigrant groups because of their political, religious, ethnic, and class differences stand in contradiction to America's stated philosophy of freedom, tolerance, and opportunity for all.

When we speak of current violence in our society today, we usually mean violence by individuals against *individuals,* rather than the more organized violence against groups that we experienced in the past. Violence in the United States can be seen in our homicide rates and numbers, in the number of child abuse cases brought to the attention of authorities, the number of domestic violence cases in the form of homicides, rapes, and assaults. The number of random or "stranger" murders and attacks has increased by almost 25% just since 1984.

What is causing such widespread and lethal violence in the United States? Many experts believe that the American fascination with guns contributes to our high homicide rates. Indeed, our country's myths and legends, built around the Wild West as well as the gangster, center on the gun and its power. The early settlers brought with them their muskets; it is said that "America was born with the rifle in its hand."16

While the perils of pioneer life were real, those dangers are gone, and yet the United States still stands out from other countries in its refusal to give up personal use of firearms. In our culture, possessing a gun is still equated by many with possessing courage or manhood. For some, particularly for juveniles, it enhances their importance, their status, their "badness." Charles Silberman, noted criminologist, illustrates how pervasive references are in our language to the gun: "the coward is gun-shy, the forthright man is a straight shooter, and the methodical person makes every shot count. While the impulsive person shoots from the hip and the impatient goes off half-cocked, the prudent man keeps his powder dry."17 Perhaps it is no coincidence that the same country that has made at least 21 movies about Billy the Kid and no fewer than nine about gangster Al Capone should have the highest rate of death from firearms as well. In Chapter Three, we will examine in depth the extent of both violent and property crime in America today.

Notes
1. Elliot Currie, *Confronting Crime: An American Challenge* (New York: Pantheon Books, 1985), pg. 5.
2. John Leo, "Crime," *Time*, June 30, 1975, pg. 45.
3. Benjamin Capps, *The Old West: The Indians* (New York: Time-Life Books, 1973), pg. 50.
4. Henry C. Dennis, *The American Indian 1492–1972: A Chronology and Fact Book* (Dobbs Ferry, N.Y.: Oceans Publications, 1977), pg. xiii.
5. Ronald H. Baily, *Violence and Aggression* (New York: Time-Life Books, 1976), pg. 107.
6. Charles Silberman, *Criminal Violence, Criminal Justice* (New York: Random House, 1978), pg. 25.
7. Carl Safikis, ed., *Encyclopedia of American Crime*. Vol. 3 (New York: Facts On File, Inc., 1981), pg. 370.
8. Samuel Walker, *Popular Justice: A History of American Criminal Justice* (New York: Oxford University Press, 1980), pg. 29.
9. Ibid., pg. 109.
10. Frank Browning and John Gerassi, *The American Way of Crime: From Salem to Watergate* (New York: G. P. Putnam's Sons, 1980), pg. 145.
11. Silberman, pg. 28.
12. Marianne W. Zawitz, ed., *Report to the Nation on Crime and Justice: Second Edition*, Bureau of Justice Statistics, NCJ-105506, March 1988, pg. 8.
13. Silberman, pg. 29.
14. Howard Zinn, *The Twentieth Century: A People's History* (New York: Harper & Row, Publishers, Inc., 1984), pg. 158.
15. Art Levine, "America's Youthful Bigots," *U.S. News and World Report*, May 7, 1990, pg. 59.
16. Lee B. Kennett, *The Gun in America: The Origins of a National Dilemma* (Westport, CT: Greenwood Press, 1975), pg. 34.
17. Silberman, pg. 37.

CHAPTER THREE

Modern Crime

In the United States, we make laws to regulate business practices, morality, individual and group behavior, civil rights and almost every other aspect of modern life. With so many different activities that could be defined as criminal, why it is that most of our attention and concern is focused on violent crimes?

The National Survey of Crime Severity, conducted in 1977, found that most people rate violent crime as more serious than property crime.[1] Yet violent crime is far less common than other kinds of crime; in fact, the number of property crimes outnumber violent crimes by about nine to one and the likelihood of being a victim of a property crime is also much greater.

We learned in Chapter One that the FBI defines homicide, forcible rape, robbery, assault, burglary, larceny-theft, motor-vehicle theft, and arson as serious crimes. In this chapter we will look more closely at some general characteristics of those crimes, including how often they are committed and how many people are arrested for them, who the victims are, and specific characteristics of the crime. In the second half of this chapter, we will examine activities that constitute white-collar or corporate crime and address the ethical and moral issues facing government and business today.

Crime Index Offenses

(All figures and definitions, except where noted, are extracted from the FBI's Uniform Crime Reports for the year 1988. The combination of this arrest data and information revealed to the National Crime Survey, which analyzes victims' perceptions of the offender and the circumstances of the crime, present the most reliable information presently available.)

Violent Crimes
Homicide

Murder is defined as "the willful killing of one human being by another." For most of us, the act of murder is both inconceivable and familiar at the same time. The number of murders we watch on television every day, the number of murder mysteries we read, and the attention we give to highly publicized murder cases reflect the fascination we have with this crime.

But for urban dwellers, particularly children, who actually witness brutal murder and shootings, this is not a fascinating or interesting crime—it is a terrible fact of life. In 1987, when the mayor of Washington D.C., Marion Barry, asked an 8th grade classroom how many knew someone who had been murdered, 14 of 19 children raised their hands. Researchers in Baltimore, Maryland recently completed a study of 168 teenagers at a local health clinic that revealed 24% of these youngsters had actually witnessed a murder and 72% knew someone who had been murdered.[2]

Though murder or homicide accounts for only 1% of violent crime and less than that of all Index offenses, it is regarded as the most serious crime by the public and is often used to gauge the extent of other crimes in the country. Homicide has the highest rate of report, highest arrest and conviction rate, receives the most severe punishment, and has one of the lowest recidivism, or repeat, rates. Though each homicide is different, there are some common characteristics and trends in the United States today.

Many cities with drug problems are experiencing increases in the number of homicides in their areas; in fact, the majority of homicides in our large cities are thought to be drug-related. The drug trade is rife with violence; drug traffickers protect their investments and territory with terror and large arsenals of weapons. While many victims are also involved in drug trafficking, some are innocent bystanders caught in the crossfire.

Almost half of the homicide victims in 1988 were black; as blacks comprise only about 12% of America's population, this high rate of victimization is of grave concern. Homicide is now the leading cause of death for black men aged 15 to 34; blacks are five times more likely than whites to be a victim of murder.[3] Homicide is a crime that does not often cross color lines: 94% of black victims were killed by black assailants and 86% of whites by whites.

More than half of all murder victims were between the ages of 20 and 34 and even young children are not immune to violent death. In fact, murder is now the leading cause of death for children in many of our inner cities.[4]

More than half of all murder victims know their assailants. In fact, many are killed by their own husbands, wives, or other family members. Domestic violence is not a new occurrence, but researchers are finding that the level of violence has increased, that more women are actually being killed or very seriously injured now than in the past as a result of attacks by their spouses or men with whom they are acquainted. Nine out of 10 women were killed by men. Almost one-third were murdered by their husbands or boyfriends.

While it's true that half of all homicide victims are killed by people they know, there are murders in which the victims were either strangers to their assailant (12%) or the relationship was unknown to police (32%). Some murders of this type occur during the commission of another crime such as a robbery or a rape.

While most murders involve one victim and one assailant, a small but frightening percentage of "stranger" homicides are committed by serial or mass murderers. The United States currently experiences about three mass murders or serial killings a month.[5]

Serial killings usually involve one offender who, sometimes over a span of years, is responsible for the murder of several, sometimes scores of people. According to Levin and Fox, researchers of the phenomenon, almost all serial murder is sexually motivated.[6] The offender profile is a white male in his late 20s or 30s, and usually is someone who has had little contact with police in the past. He often suffers from psychological problems, such as sociopathy or, more infrequently, paranoid schizophrenia.

Sociopaths are people who suffer a character disorder that impairs their ability to feel empathy, guilt, or morality. The law does not view sociopaths as mentally ill. Many serial killers, such as Ted Bundy, John William Gacy, and Henry Lee Lucas successfully eluded police for years and together were responsible for hundreds of murders. These crimes, carried out over long periods of time, are often difficult to solve and, ironically, many of these killers are caught not as a result of police investigation, but in connection with other offenses, such as traffic violations. Ted Bundy, who may have killed as many as 100 women, for instance, was caught after being stopped by police for running a stop sign on a suburban street in Florida.

Unlike serial killings, mass murders involve the killing of four or more victims at a single location. For example, Charles Whitman climbed to a tower at the University of Texas and killed 16 people with his rifle on August 1, 1966, and Oliver Huberty shot 21 people to death at a MacDonald's in San Diego in 1984; these are just two horrifying examples of homicidal

rage. Usually impulsive rather than well-thought-out or calcu-
lated acts, mass murders are believed to be the culmination of
lifelong feelings of powerlessness and failure.

Almost half of those arrested for murder in 1988 were between the ages of 20 and 34. Though juvenile arrests for this
crime showed an increase of about 50% from 1984 to 1988,
juveniles actually account for a very small percentage of the
total arrests for murder.[7] Nearly 90% of those arrested for
murder in 1988 were male and 53% were black.

Murder can be the result of passion or an argument that is
out of control; calculation, such as premeditated execution by
organized crime or the planned murder of a spouse; and mental
illness, as in the cases of the mass murderer or serial killer. It is
estimated that about one-third of all homicides are the result of
an argument of some kind. In less than one-fourth of the cases,
the crime is committed in conjunction with another felony, such
as robbery or a drug transaction.

By far the majority of homicide victims are killed by firearms.
Publicity and concern about the number of assault weapons
bought and sold in the United States has sparked much debate
and even community bans on this type of weapon. Handguns,
however, remain the number one firearm used in murders.

Assault

Aggravated assault is defined as an attack "for the purpose
of inflicting serious or aggravated bodily injury" and is usually
accomplished through the "use of a weapon or by means likely
to produce death or great bodily harm." Aggravated assault by
definition is an attack so serious that it could result in death.

Assault accounts for 67% of violent crime and 7% of all Index
offenses. The 33% increase since 1985 in arrests for this crime is
another indication of the rising level of violence in the country.
The number of juvenile arrests are also cause for concern; these
have increased by almost 30% in the last four years.

A crime that usually involves one victim and one assailant, assault is committed most often in the summer months when heat and other environmental conditions strain the senses. It is a violent crime, committed most often with blunt objects or personal weapons such as fists or feet. Knives and guns each account for about 20% of assaults; assaults with guns increased by about 10% from 1987 to 1988.

Rape

The Uniform Crime Reports defines rape as "the carnal knowledge of a female forcibly and against her will." By this definition, all rape victims are female; although men are also victims of sexual assault, such crimes are rarely reported. According to the National Crime Survey of 1985, over half of the female rape victims were under the age of 25 and most often the crime was committed between the hours of 6:00 P.M. and 6:00 A.M.

Until fairly recently, the crime of rape was vastly under-reported, particularly in the cases where the victim and assailant knew each other. Many women did not call the police because they felt ashamed or had some doubts that their case could be brought to court. Some could not face reliving the trauma of the experience nor stand up to being questioned publically in court.

In the past, many women suffered further indignity at the hands of often insensitive police and a brutal court system. Court proceedings questioned the victim's relationship with the offender, her sexual history, as well as such details as the clothing she was wearing at the time of the rape. Recent rulings, however prohibit reviewing a woman's sexual history in court. In addition, most every police department now has special rape counselors on staff to ease the process for traumatized victims.

The term "date rape" refers to an incident of forced sexual relations with an acquaintance. Researchers believe that at least one-fourth of college women have had this experience, but many have been reluctant to report it. In addition to feelings of anger, the victims of this type of sexual assault may also feel a great deal of confusion, shame, and guilt about the incident. More women, however, are beginning to step forward and successfully prosecute men who expect and force sex on their companions, girlfriends, wives, or acquaintances.

Robbery

Robbery is considered a violent crime because it involves "force or the threat of force or violence and/or putting the victim in fear." Sometimes called a mugging or a stick-up, this crime accounts for 35% of violent crime and 4% of total Crime Index offenses.

A full 59% of those arrested for this crime in 1988 were under the age of 25, 63% were black, and 92% were men. Strongarm tactics are most often the type of force used during this crime, but a full one-third of robberies reported were committed by robbers using handguns. Many robberies are carried out in combination with other crimes such as rape, murder, and assault. It is a crime most often committed by strangers and more often than other crimes involves more than one assailant.

Reported losses from robberies in the United States in 1988 were about $343 million; the average incident netted the assailant about $631.

Property Crimes

The crimes of burglary, larceny-theft, motor vehicle theft, and arson are classified as property crimes because they do not involve personal injury or the threat of injury. They make up the majority of both the Crime Index arrests and offenses. For these offenses, the offender characteristics are somewhat different than those of violent crimes. The majority of those arrested are white, and the average age of the offender is lower than that of the violent offender.

Burglary

Burglary is the "unlawful entry of a structure to commit a felony or theft" and represents 26% of all property crimes. In two out of three burglaries, residential property was the target. Nationally, about $3.3 billion was lost as a result of burglaries in 1988; the average residential burglary netted about $1,014 and the average nonresidential $967 for the criminal.

Larceny-theft

Larceny-theft is the "unlawful taking, carrying, leading, or riding away of property from the possession" of another person. Purse-snatching, shoplifting, pickpocketing, and thefts from cars are some of the methods included in this category. Arrests for this offense account for over half of all Crime Index offense arrests and a full 70% of all property arrests. In terms of crimes reported to police, larceny-theft accounts for most of the crimes reported. In an average incident, about $426 is stolen. Altogether, about $3.3 billion is stolen each year during the commission of larceny-thefts. Since the victim often does not even report the crime, these figures are probably much higher.

Interestingly, women were arrested for larceny-theft more often than for any other crime. Sixty-three percent of those arrested were white and 32% were black. Of all those arrested, 44% were under 21, 30% were under 18.

Motor Vehicle Theft

Another common property crime is the theft of motor vehicles, including automobiles, trucks, buses, motorcycles, and snowmobiles. The average loss equaled about $5,117 per vehicle, or $7 billion nationally. Fifty-eight percent of those arrested were under the age of 21 and almost half were under the age of 18. Most of the offenders were white males.

How Much Crime Is There?

If it is true that only one-third of all crime committed is actually reported, and if only a small proportion of those crimes reported are cleared by arrest, then the number of crimes and criminals in this country is truly staggering. The following chart represents the *estimated* total arrests made in 1988 according to the latest Uniform Crime Report:

Total Estimated Arrests 1988

Total	13,812,300

Part I Offenses

Murder	21,890
Forcible rape	38,610
Robbery	149,100
Aggravated assault	416,300
Burglary	463,400
Larceny-theft	1,571,200
Motor vehicle theft	208,400
Arson	19,700

Part II Offenses

Other assaults	901,800
Forgery and counterfeiting	101,700
Fraud	366,300
Embezzlement	15,500
Stolen property; buying, receiving, possessing	166,300
Vandalism	295,300
Weapons; carrying, possessing, etc.	221,800
Prostitution and commercialized vice	104,100
Sex offenses (except forcible rape/ prostitution)	106,300
Drug abuse violations	1,155,200
Gambling	23,600
Offenses against family and children	69,900
Driving under the influence	1,792,500
Liquor laws	669,600
Drunkenness	818,600
Disorderly conduct	760,500

Total Estimated Arrests 1988

Vagrancy	36,500
All other offenses (except traffic)	3,078,900
Suspicion (not included in totals)	14,000
Curfew and loitering laws	72,200
Runaways	166,900

It is wise to keep in mind that most studies reveal that "most serious crimes are committed by a relatively small number of criminals, who tend to repeat their offenses despite frequent spells of imprisonment."[8]

"Victimless" Crimes

If we define a crime as an offense against society, then there can be no true crimes without victims. Society defines certain acts as criminal in part because they offend the sensibility or morality of the majority; when they are committed, they are assumed to offend all of us even when no one but the offender is involved. That is the view of the legislators who have made gambling, prostitution, homosexuality, drug use, drunkenness, vagrancy, and obscenity punishable crimes.

Though most of these crimes are punishable only by fines and not imprisonment, they account for a large proportion of Part II arrests. Some argue that since these are acts committed without coercion, force, violence, and with the consent of those involved, they should not be considered criminal. In these crimes, the offender and the victim are often the same person. This is not the case when children are involved because, by definition, children are not of the age of consent.

Those who advocate the legalization or government regulation of this type of crime argue that making such acts criminal creates an underground and potentially violent subculture. Further, the criminalization of these acts does little to deter the offender from committing them. Is it fair that some forms of gambling, such as the stock market, are legal while others are not? If addiction and public health are the issues, why are cigarettes and alcohol legal and not drugs?

The related crime and violence of the drug trade would be eliminated, say advocates of legalization of drugs such as William F. Buckley, if drugs were not in the hands of criminals. Drug abuse then could be prevented or treated through early education and treatment, in much the same way alcohol abuse is, instead of through the criminal justice system.

Prostitution is another example of a victimless crime. Saving the victim from herself through prosecution has not stopped the practice of exchanging money for sex and, further, the men who pay for the service are not arrested at the same rate as the prostitutes themselves.

Reducing the number of acts that are considered criminal might go a long way towards reducing crime statistics. The money saved in the criminal justice system and in law enforcement might be better spent by funding prevention or treatment programs.

Opponents of legalization strongly argue that decriminalizing these activities, especially in the case of drug use, would condone the act, increase the availability of the goods and services, and therefore increase the number of participants. If, for example, drugs were available through prescription for those over 21, many who previously had been deterred from drug use because of the criminality of the act would feel more free to use drugs. Furthermore, a black market for underage or ineligible recipients, critics argue, would not be completely eliminated. The ongoing struggle to curb the drug trade and drug abuse in the United States will undoubtedly inspire further heated debate on such controversial solutions.

White-Collar Crime

Publicity about violent crime can obscure the seriousness of other types of crimes. Robbery and burglary are well-known phenomena, but embezzlement, though committed without violence, usually involves more monetary gain than the typical robbery or burglary. In 1985, for example, among the white-collar cases referred to the U.S. Attorney General more than 140 people were charged with offenses estimated to involve over $1 million each and 64 were charged with offenses valued at over $10 million each. In the same year, losses from all bank robberies were under $19 million and losses from all robberies were about $313 million. White-collar crimes may not involve violence, but they cost the country billions of dollars a year.[9]

White-collar crime is not a legal crime classification, but a category of offenses with common characteristics. Originally used to refer to the offender, to distinguish him or her from working-class or "blue-collar" criminals, the term is now used to describe the type of offenses rather than the person who commits them. The Department of Justice defines white-collar crime as "those nonviolent offenses which principally involve elements of deceit, deception, concealment, corruption, misrepresentation, and a breach of trust," or more simply, "nonviolent crime for financial gain committed by deception."[10]

The crimes for which one would be prosecuted under this category are: forgery and counterfeiting, fraud, and embezzlement. There are numerous criminal activities that might lead to prosecution of these four offenses, including price-fixing, manufacture and sale of harmful foods and drugs, water and air pollution, bribery, data theft, computer tampering, and inside trading.

Because of the difficulty in uncovering these crimes and the typically high economic status of the offender, it has been common for offenders to either avoid prosecution altogether or be treated in a more lenient manner than other kinds of nonviolent criminals, like burglars or larcenists. In recent years, the nature and extent of the crimes committed by the businessperson, government official, or stock trader has brought this discrepency to the attention of the public and law enforcement officials. Although sentences for white-collar crimes have increased in recent years, critics claim that, considering the potential profit to be gained, the offender still is undeterred.

Because many businesses do not report wrongdoing and individuals who are victims of white-collar crime may be too embarrassed to report the offense, or may never discover the crime, it is difficult to calculate exactly how much money is lost as a direct result of white-collar crime. Estimates range from $40 to $100 billion a year.

One of the central issues regarding white-collar crime concerns ethics in business, that is, what the line is between fair and standard business practice and fraud and corruption. How far can those in positions of power go in order to get ahead, either personally or for the sake of the company before they are committing a crime? Though some unethical practices in business and government—bribery, kickbacks, price-fixing, and insider trading, for instance—may have been accepted as standard business practice in some companies in the past, these activities are now under more scrutiny, from both the authorized regulatory commissions and the American public.

How far is too far? The law states that it is illegal to accept a money in exchange for a lucrative contract for the company. Is it also wrong to accept an expensive bottle of champagne from a friendly vendor? When does a friendly or generous gesture become a bribe? When does a stock market tip become information gained through illegal means? These are some of the questions we will be examining in this look at white-collar crime.

Corporate Crime

How corrupt are our businesses? From 1975 to 1984, 62% of America's Fortune 500 corporations were cited for one or more illegal activities. There are two types of business or corporate crime; one type is committed by individuals for personal gain and another is committed by a corporation or agency through its business practices for corporate gain. The bank employee who embezzles funds does so for personal gain; a bank that knowingly launders drug money does so for corporate or government gain.

Fraud is a category that covers a broad range of activities. The U.S. Justice Department includes tax fraud, lending and credit fraud, wire fraud, and other fraud in this category. Other fraud covers false claims and statements; government program fraud; fraud concerning bankruptcy, commodities, securities, passports, or citizenship; and conspiracy to defraud.

Trading on Wall Street

What is the difference between a good tip on the stock market and one that is gotten through illegal means? Many stockbrokers are finding out that the difference is actually clearly stated in the law and those who disregard the law are finding themselves in the federal courts. Insider trading, which is trading stocks based on confidential information regarding corporate takeovers, is an illegal activity that has been common practice at many stock exchange companies.

The recent case involving Drexel Burnham Lambert Inc., a brokerage house on Wall Street, is a good example of the intricate web of deception spun for individual profit. When Dennis Levine, an employee in the merger department was arrested on May 12, 1986, he was charged with gaining $12 million in illegal profits from confidential information regarding upcoming corporate takeovers. When caught, Levine went undercover for the U.S. Attorney General's office and obtained evidence against another trader, Ivan Boesky. This investigation opened up a huge inside-trading scandal that continues to effect stock market houses across the nation.

Even though the case against Boesky was not strong—the most serious charge he faced was conspiracy to file false documents—Boesky was eager to make a deal with authorities. He agreed to plead guilty to the current charge, pay a fine of $100 million, and provide information about other traders involved to the FBI. He taped incriminating conversations with colleagues, even going so far as to wear a wire at a Beverly Hills party, and led authorities to Martin Siegel, from whom it is estimated that Boesky made over $32 million from illegal information, and to Michael Milken, the now infamous junk-bond king.

Government Corruption

One of the biggest scandals to be revealed in recent years involved the U.S. Department of Defense. The Pentagon spends approximately $160 billion a year in materials ranging from sophisticated weapons to ordinary supplies. Purchasing and receiving purchase orders is a big business for the Defense Department; 15 million contracts are given out each year. A Presidential Commission appointed to reform the procedure called the procurement system "fundamentally ill" and a two-year investigation of fraud and bribery that began in 1986 called Operation Ill Wind, revealed widespread corruption.

In the course of this investigation, it was discovered that a significant number of contracts were obtained based on inside information and awarded in exchange for money or gifts. One investigator claimed that "there hasn't been a significant contract let in the past six or eight years that hasn't been made on the basis of inside information."[11] As a result of Operation Ill Wind, a number of high-ranking Pentagon officials as well as executives from such corporations as Teledyne and McDonnell-Douglass either pled guilty or were convicted by the courts.

Corporate Violence

Corporate violence is a fairly new term that refers to business practices that some claim endanger public safety and cause thousands of unnecessary deaths each year. Estimates run as high as 100,000 deaths a year resulting from poorly distributed and manufactured products.12 Though controversial, the idea that corporations can be held criminally responsible for endangering the public is gaining credence as more criminal cases are being brought against corporations. Cases against the tobacco industry, for example, charge that the industry knowingly manufactured a deadly product. When a company knowingly dumps hazardous waste, it endangers the health and safety of thousands of citizens. It is believed that more criminal cases against corporations will be prosecuted.

Although criminal charges against corporations have increased in number, it is far more common for corporations to be charged with civil rather than criminal complaints. Since the standard of proof in criminal cases is much higher than in civil cases, civil sanctions in the form of fines are most often sought in cases against corporations.

In Corporate Crime and Violence, author Russell Mokhiber documents 36 cases involving large corporations. These include the owners of the nuclear power plant Three Mile Island, Ford Motor Corporation, Nestle, Firestone, and General Motors. The author documents cases which, he claims, demonstrate how corporate greed and lax standards can result in injury and death. He further claims that the judicial system protects big business from criminal prosecution, while holding individuals more accountable for similar offenses.

Unsafe working conditions, including exposure to deadly chemicals or substandard equipment, cause injury and death to thousands of unsuspecting employees. Although such cases are rare, corporations that knowingly endanger the lives of workers have been charged with negligent homicide.

Telemarketing Fraud

The telemarketing industry sells over $100 billion a year in legitimate goods and services. But the Federal Trade Commission estimates that at least another billion dollars is given to fraudulent individuals and phony companies that promise consumers products or services they don't deliver.

Conducting stock bond trades, selling vacation homes and fine art, these criminals use telephone sales to bilk consumers by insisting that purchases be made with a credit card. Their insistence on the credit card serves two functions: the con artist can cash the credit card voucher before the consumer can change his or her mind and, further, he or she can use the card number to charge the customer for other purchases. About $105 million were lost in this type of credit card fraud in 1989.

Individuals from the Federal Trade Commission, consumers, businesspeople, securities regulators, and bankers have joined together to form the Alliance Against Fraud in Telemarketing in an effort to pressure Congress for legislation aimed at regulating the telemarketing industry.

Computers have become the new method of choice for an old-fashioned crime: Gone are the days of masked men sticking up bank tellers; today, computer technology has opened up new windows of opportunity for enterprising thieves. Nearly one trillion dollars are transferred from bank accounts through electronic wires each year, and though banks have attempted to prevent the illegal transfer of funds, huge sums of money are being stolen every year by talented computer thieves.

An employee in the wire transfer office at the Chicago Bank and five accomplices, for instance, managed to transfer $69 million from the accounts of three major corporations into a bank account in Vienna, Austria. The unlucky crew was caught before withdrawing the money from Vienna when one company was notified that its account was overdrawn. If the thieves had not taken such a huge sum of money, their crimes might never have been detected.

While sophisticated technology may deter the more old-fashioned bank robbers, it can also provide the tools for the computer-literate employee to steal enormous sums of money. Indeed, illegal electronic transfers may soon replace traditional bank robberies.

The crimes committed by government, businesses, and through new computer technology are no less serious than other property crimes. Historically, however, those accused of these crimes have fared better in our judicial system: Sentences are often lighter than for other property crimes and conviction rates are lower. As more cases come to the attention of the courts and the American public, these discrepancies will hopefully disappear. Equality before the law is necessary if Americans are to have faith in our system of justice.

Victims of Crime in the United States

What are the chances of becoming a victim of a crime in modern America? While it is not possible to tell anyone with complete certainty whether he or she will be a victim, the National Crime Survey (NCS) has devised formulas that calculate the likelihood of becoming a victim.

The NCS, in its "Lifetime Likelihood of Victimization," published in 1987, estimates that five out of six people in the United States will become victims of a violent crime at some point in their lives, men more than women, and about half of the population will have this experience more than once. Nearly everyone in this country will at some time become a victim of personal theft, and seven out of eight people will be victimized three or more times. As one gets older, however, the likelihood of becoming a victim decreases dramatically, especially of violent crimes.

According to this publication, almost 4,000,000 households and people over the age of 12 were victims of crime in 1988. Who are the most likely victims of crime? According to the NCS, those who are male, poor, young, and inner city residents are more likely than other groups to be victims of crime. Blacks in this country are often in one or more of these risk groups and, indeed, are more often victims of crime than other groups, especially for rape, robbery, and aggravated assault. In reviewing responses from Hispanics versus non-Hispanics, Hispanics reported more than double the robbery rate.

The chances of becoming a victim of violent crime decreases as family income increases, while personal theft crimes, however, increase as wealth and property accumulate. In general, people under 25 were more likely than older people to become crime victims.

According to this study, then, to be young, poor, a member of a minority group, or a city dweller increases the chances of becoming the target of criminal behavior. For each crime category, blacks sustained more victimization than whites, and Hispanics more than non-Hispanics.

This victimization is in part due to the high crime rate in our large cities. The increase in both violent and property crimes our cities are experiencing is considered to be a direct result of the illegal drug trade. In Chapter Four, we will address the relationship between drug use and trafficking and other types of crime.

Notes

1. Marianne W. Zawitz, ed., *Report to the Nation on Crime and Justice: Second Edition*, Bureau of Justice Statistics, NCJ-105506, March 1988, pg. 16.
2. Karl Zinsmeister, "Growing Up Scared," *The Atlantic*, June 1990, pg. 50.

3. Susan Tifft, "Fighting the Failure Syndrome," *Time*, May 21, 1990, pg. 83.
4. Op. cit., pg. 51
5. Jack Levin and James Fox, *Mass Murder: America's New Menace.* (New York: Plenum Press, 1985), pg. 20.
6. Ibid, pg. 67.
7. U.S. Department of Justice, *Uniform Crime Report 1988* (Washington D.C.: Federal Bureau of Investigation, August 1989), pg. 174.
8. *Crime: What We Fear, What Can Be Done*, prepared by the Public Agenda Foundation, National Issues Forum, 1986, pg. 1.
9. U.S. Department of Justice, *Federal Offenses and Offenders: White Collar Crime*, Bureau of Justice Statistics, NCJ-106876, September, 1987, pg. 1.
10. U.S. Department of Justice, *Tracking White Collar Criminals*, Bureau of Justice Statistics, November 1986, pg. 2.
11. Ed Magnunson, "The Pentagon For Sale," *Time*, June 27, 1988, pg. 16.
12. Joan Claybrook, "White Collar Crime Boom," *Public Citizen*, August 1985, pg. 5.

CHAPTER FOUR

Drugs and Crime

The National Institute for Drug Abuse (NIDA) estimates that approximately 56,000,000 people have smoked marijuana, 22,000,000 have used cocaine, and that there are at least 500,000 heroin addicts in the United States.[1] In fact, the United States has the highest level of "psychoactive drug use of any industrialized society." By some estimates, users in this country spend about $50 billion a year in illegal drugs, $20 billion on cocaine.[2] During the past decade drug use, drug arrests, and drug-related crime have all increased.

Many experts point to the emergence of cocaine, especially the very recent availability of a cheap and more addictive form of the drug—crack—an alarming increase in heroin use, and various social and economic factors as the reasons for the upsurge in drug abuse for some portions of the population. The economic cost of our drug problem is enormous; the amount of human suffering, for both the individual user and his or her family, is tragic. It is estimated that treatment is available for only 260,000 of the more than two million drug users in need of help,[3] that 60% of New York City's heroin addicts are infected with the deadly AIDS virus,[4] and that crack cocaine has a stranglehold on our inner cities.

In addition, many experts believe that the rise in drug abuse is directly related to a rise in other crimes: murder, assault, robbery, rape, and child abuse are just some of the painful side-effects of the abuse of serious drugs.

At the same time that drug use has increased to 10 to 30 times the level of 20 years ago, there have been some very recent changes in drug use in the country.[5] According to reports by the NIDA, there has been a decrease in the total amount of drug use in the population: use of all illicit drugs has decreased 37% since 1985. As reported in a NIDA 1988 survey, those who claimed to use marijuana on a monthly basis dropped from 18,000,000 to 11,600,000; those using heroin, according to this survey, remained stable at 500,000, and those using cocaine dropped from 5,800,000 to 2,900,000, a decrease of 50% from 1985.[6]

This trend is also supported by the NIDA's 1989 High School Senior Survey of Drug Abuse, which shows declines in drug use for both high-school seniors and young adults. Both current use (use within the last 30 days) and lifetime use of cocaine and marijuana showed decline; lifetime, annual, and current use of crack remained the same, and PCP, the only drug that showed an increase in use, showed increases in both current use (up from 0.3% in 1988 to 1.4% 1989) and annual use (up from 1.2% to 2.4%). (This trend is particularly worrisome because PCP, a hallucinogen, is a very dangerous drug. Some of the side effects associated with PCP use include depression, bizarre and violent behavior, and permanent brain dysfunction.) In general, however, annual and current use of all illicit drugs declined for high school seniors as well as for young adults, a group which historically has the largest number of drug users in the society.

The survey did indicate, however, that half of all high school seniors will have tried an illicit drug before graduation and that, despite intensive educational campaigns aimed at the high school population, no changes were reported regarding alcohol use. Further, although these figures indicate that casual use of drugs has decreased, the number of weekly or daily regular users of drugs, especially cocaine, has increased in the last five years.

The majority of arrests for drug violations are for marijuana, cocaine, and heroin. Each comes from plants that are indigenous to specific countries or areas; of the three, only marijuana is grown in the United States.

Heroin

During the past decade there has been such an increase in cocaine and cocaine trafficking that little is heard about heroin anymore. Does this mean that we've succeeded in reducing either the amount of heroin available or the demand for it? On the contrary, approximately seven to eight tons of heroin are consumed each year in the United States at a street value of approximately $20 billion.[7]

The federal Drug Enforcement Agency, which is responsible for the regulation of drugs in the United States, claims that the heroin addict population has remained steady at 500,000, the same figure that President Nixon cited when he first made heroin use a national issue in 1971. But there are some who argue that both the flow of heroin and the crime organization responsible for its trafficking have been allowed to grow as drug enforcement officials focused their attention on the cocaine trade. Many drug experts believe that the number of heroin users may be rising for the first time in years.

Both heroin and the drug morphine are manufactured from raw opium, a drug extracted from the poppy plant. When the brilliantly colored petals of the poppy flower fall off, a green seed pod is left, which produces a thick sap. This sap is raw opium. In the hills of Southeast Asia, from Burma to Laos, hundreds of thousands of acres of poppies are planted and cultivated by farmers.

The amount of opium extracted from each pod is very small, about the size of a pea. Laboratories set up in the mountains or jungles transform opium into morphine. The transformation necessary to then turn morphine into heroin requires more sophisticated labs, often located in Europe or Hong Kong.

The largest producer of opium is an area called the Golden Triangle, which is located in Southeast Asia and includes parts of Thailand, Laos, and Burma. A good crop here might yield 1,500 tons of raw opium and more than half of that will be exported as morphine or heroin. The second largest producer of opium products is an area in the Middle East that includes the countries of Afghanistan, Pakistan, and Iran, and is referred to as the "Golden Crescent." This area produces about 600 tons of opium; but only 15% leaves the country—the rest is consumed by the local addict population.

For hundreds of years opium has been a part of the culture of the hill tribes who cultivate the poppy. Seen as a gift from the gods, it is used in cooking, it is eaten, smoked, and used in tribal ceremonies, offered as part of a bride's dowry, and often given as payment to farmers by drug traffickers. Addiction among the tribes runs high, providing further motivation for continued cultivation by the farmers.

Opium Use in the United States

Opium use in this country most likely began after the introduction of Dover's Powder, a remedy developed by an English physician by the name of Thomas Dover in 1709. Its ingredients included equal parts of opium, ipecac, and licorice, combined with saltpeter, tartar, and wine.[8]

Dover's Powder began a trend in the United States; soon medicines and elixirs containing opium were plentiful and readily available from druggists and grocers. Many of the users were from the middle and upper class who took their "remedies" daily. Such products as Mrs. Winlow's Soothing Syrup, Godfrey's Cordial, and Scott's Emulsion were marketed as "women's friends" and "soothing syrups" and were hailed as cures for a variety of ailments, including athlete's foot, dysentery, cold, and even cancer.

In 1803 morphine, the main byproduct of opium, was discovered by a German pharmacist. It was named after Morpheus, the Greek God of dreams, and has become the most widely used and effective painkiller in history. In 1831 two dozen other opium alkaloids were discovered; experiments combining various acids with morphine led British chemist C.R.A. Wright to develop a new substance called diacetylmorphine. Bayer and Company successfully marketed this drug in a dozen countries under the name heroin, meaning heroic and powerful in German. Hailed as a miracle drug, it was one of the world's most widely prescribed drugs, promoted as a remedy for coughs and respiratory illnesses as well as a cure for morphine addiction.

By the turn of the century, there were about 50,000 medicines containing opiates available in drugstores in the country. When Congress passed the Harrison Act in 1914 to restrict the distribution of narcotics and cocaine, heroin was not included, but would later be banned in 1924 with the passage of the Jones-Miller Act. As the supplier of heroin changed from the local pharmacist to an illegal drug dealer, the image of a heroin user slowly changed from a "legitimate" member of society to a member of an underground subculture.

It is believed that heroin addiction had, for the most part, been eradicated by the 1940s. After World War II, when opium and heroin traffickers from Southeast Asia and Europe re-established contacts with the United States, the heroin population was primarily restricted to the inner city ghettos. For decades, the heroin population has remained fairly stable, but many sources believe that both the number and the profile of users is changing.

In his book, *Warlords of Crime*, author Gerald Posner documents his theories about the increase of heroin use and trafficking in the United States. He contends that our heroin population has actually increased from 500,000 to 750,000, a figure also supported by the U.S. Department of Justice.[9] Today, mixing heroin with cocaine has become prevalent for casual as well as regular cocaine users. Known as "chasing the dragon," crack users mix and smoke the drugs to reduce the intensity of the cocaine. It is believed that the practice is gaining popularity in Hollywood circles. Smoking heroin removes the stigma and dangers attached to needles and is giving a wider, younger population a taste for the drug.

Posner contends that the newest group controlling the heroin flow here is a network of Chinese organized crime syndicates called the triads. Originating in China in the late 17th century, these secret societies are now seen as a major threat to efforts to stem the flow of heroin to the United States. Posner quotes Jon Elder, police chief from Monterey Park, California: "Asian organized crime will end up being the number one organized crime problem in North America in the next five years. In my humble opinion, they'll make the Sicilian Mafia look like a bunch of Sunday school kids".[10]

It appears that others have anticipated an increase in demand for heroin—it has been discovered that opium is now being grown in Llanos, a remote area of Colombia, and domestic opium was discovered in 1985 during a raid on marijuana fields in Vermont. Here officials discovered 2,000 opium plants with their pods already sliced open.[11] Senator Joseph Biden stated that "we are on the verge of another heroin epidemic that may be the worst in United States history."[12]

Cocaine and Crack

The NIDA reports that the population of regular cocaine users, those who used cocaine weekly, has increased from 647,000 to 862,000 during the last five years. Other researchers, however, believe that the government's household survey has underestimated larger cocaine use in the inner city.

Cocaine is an alkaloid, a member of a group of plants that produce substances such as nicotine, caffeine, and morphine. The coca shrub, of which there are two varieties, is primarily found in the Andean Valley in South America; in fact, 90% of all the coca leaves in the world are grown in Peru and Bolivia. Historically, the ancient Incas believed that the plant was of divine origin; its use was a symbol of high social rank or order; the casual chewing of coca leaves was considered a sacrilege. Today however, many of the thousands of farmers who culti- vate the coca chew the leaves and use them in cooking as well as in religious ceremonies. Many are addicted to the drug.

Thousands of years after the Incas, European explorers brought back tales of a wonderful new drug that produced both feelings of euphoria as well as increased energy and stimula- tion. In the late 1700s, Angleo Mariani of Corsica concocted a combination of extracts from imported coca leaves and wine to produce a new beverage—Vin Coca Mariani. The drink in- duced a feeling of general well-being and was advertised as a cure for fatigue. Mariani's great success with his wine inspired John Styth Pemberton to manufacture a similar product: He called it Coca Cola, and it allegedly contained a small amount of the "real thing."

It wasn't until 1860 that the alkaloid cocaine was first ex- tracted from the coca leaves. When a supply of this form of coca produced increased energy and productivity when it was given to German soldiers, the medical profession became interested in the drug's stimulating effects. Sigmund Freud, noted Aus- trian psychiatrist, used cocaine extensively to combat chronic fatigue and depression; he also recommended it as a cure for morphine addiction.

Cocaine was hailed as a miracle drug and by 1890 was added to the growing number of home remedies and medicines in the United States. In 1906 the Pure Food and Drug Act was passed and, while this law did not make the drug illegal, it did force the patent-medicine industry to reveal the amount of alcohol, heroin, cocaine, and morphine in its products. Growing public concern and information regarding the dangers of these drugs, in particular their addictive qualities, lead to a decline in these over-the-counter products. When the Harrison Act of 1914 was passed, cocaine officially went underground and its use was not widespread for decades.

Cocaine again gained popularity during the 1980s, a decade that stressed high achievement and fast money. Cocaine was the perfect accompaniment for this life-style, and became the recreational drug of choice for a growing young professional population. An expensive drug that stimulates the nervous system and produces a general feeling of power and euphoria, cocaine use was fairly widespread during this decade and was at first thought to be a safe, recreational drug, especially in contrast to the narcotic heroin.

By the mid-1980s, abuse of cocaine and new forms of the drug began to take their toll in terms of addiction and death. When speedballing—mixing and injecting heroin and cocaine—killed the comedian John Belushi and a massive dose of cocaine took the life of athlete Len Bias, cocaine's immense popularity began to wane among casual users.

The heavy user, however, found a new, inexpensive form of cocaine. Crack cocaine, which hit the United States in about 1986, is fired to release its potency, and smoked. Available for as little as $5.00 a hit, crack has become the drug of choice for some of the young people in our cities.

The South American Connection

In the Andean area of South America, cocaine has become one of the most important crops: In Bolivia, the drug cartels are said to carry more political power than the government and have more power and money than the army, and in Peru, cocaine is the county's biggest export, bringing in some $1 billion a year. Although Colombia is not a big producer of coca leaves, it is the center for manufacturing cocaine and trafficking it to the United States and other countries.

Cocaine has become Colombia's biggest national export; it is estimated that the drug earns the country from $2 to $4 billion, double the yield of coffee exports. The center of Colombia's drug trade is located in Medellin, a manufacturing city of approximately two million people and headquarters of the powerful Medellin cartel of cocaine traffickers. Because of the cocaine trade, this city is currently home to about 20,000 millionaires.

In a country torn apart by 40 years of civil strife, the Medellin cartel nevertheless stands out as the perpetrator of unbelievable violence and terror: Medellin currently experiences about 10 murders a day. Judges, police, and journalists have all been the targets of assassinations. In the spring of 1990, retaliations against officials responsible for extradicting drug traffickers to the United States have been carried out by a powerful drug cartel known as The Extradictables. After the Colombian government agreed to cooperate with the United States by sending known drug traffickers to this country to face drug charges in our courts, this group bombed residential areas of the capital, and executed judges, government officials, and newspaper personnel in retaliation.

While there are perhaps 300 "kingpins" at the top of the pyramid of the cocaine business, it is estimated that thousands of farmers, runners, and manufacturers are involved in the overall business of cocaine production and trafficking. Farmers in Colombia earn about $3.50 working traditional crops and $25.00 a day in the coca fields. In Peru, coca is the only crop for many farmers.[13]

The economic importance of cocaine production and trafficking for these countries will be considered when looking at the successes and failures of the United States drug policy at the end of this chapter.

Marijuana

According to the NIDA, some 11 million Americans smoke marijuana each month. Marijuana use in the United States increased tremendously in the 1960s, but neither the drug nor its use is new. From the hardy *Cannabis* plant, marijuana has been grown throughout the world for thousands of years. It has an intoxicating effect and has been long used in medicine as well as in religious rituals.

Apparently unaware of the plant's effects, the English exported the plant to the new American colonies, where the plant's fibrous content was used as a source for rope. Its first use as a drug in the United States was not noted until the late 1800s when physicians began publishing articles about its medicinal qualities.

While clandestine hashish clubs attracted some well-to-do clients in several large cities, its use remained fairly limited to several ethnic groups, including blacks in the South and Mexican immigrants, who brought the drug with them across the border. By the turn of the century, as the alcohol reform movement gained in strength, marijuana was negatively associated with minority groups and the campaign against its use became quite strident. Although Congress attempted to include *Cannabis* in its list of illegal drugs in 1911, this effort failed.

During Prohibition, organized crime began to import and distribute marijuana. The FBI in the 1930s began what today would be considered a hysterical campaign against the drug, claiming that its use would lead to insanity and violence.[14] Users were portrayed as promiscuous, as having associations with or being members of minority groups, and as criminals. In 1937, the Marijuana Tax Law was passed to control its use, but it was not until 1956 that marijuana was included as an illegal drug in the Federal Narcotics Act. From that time until 1970, further federal and state restrictions followed.

In the 1960s, marijuana use spread from the inner cities as young people across the nation began experimenting with the drug. Within a very short period of time, marijuana was a drug used by millions of Americans, from the children of judges, police, and corporate executives to the judges, police, and executives themselves.

By 1970, the growing population of marijuana users influenced the passage of the Comprehensive Drug Abuse Prevention and Control Act, which reduced federal penalties for possession of marijuana. In the same year, the Uniform Controlled Substance Act reclassified marijuana as an hallucinogen rather than a narcotic and reclassified possession for personal use from a felony to a misdemeanor. A majority of American states have adopted the Uniform Act and 11 states have made possession for personal use a noncriminal act, punishable by fine rather than imprisonment.

In the past, most of the marijuana sold in the United States was imported from countries such as Mexico, Colombia, Jamaica, and Thailand. Recent trends, however, show a huge increase in domestically grown marijuana. When Mexico started spraying marijuana with a dangerous herbicide called paraquat in 1978, increased domestic production as well as increased imports from other countries resulted. Today, domestically grown marijuana is a huge business and may well be one of our largest cash crops.[15]

Although historically marijuana has been associated with a young and rather peaceful user group, the big business of producing and trafficking the drug is becoming riddled with related crime and violence. In Oklahoma, where several homicides have been linked to the marijuana trade, police feel they must not relax enforcement of drug laws. One Oklahoman is quoted as saying, "If it runs away with us, we face an explosion of official and political corruption—murder for hire, larceny, corruption of the criminal-justice system. We'll be a harbinger of things to come in the United States."[16]

Though use of marijuana remains fairly widespread in the country, its use has decreased in recent years rather than increased despite both greater availability and reductions in penalties for possession.

Drug Use and Crime

How does the use of drugs lead to criminal activity? The most direct relationship is seen in the number of actual drug law violations; in 1988, that figure stood at over one million. First, the possession of illegal drugs is a crime. The possession with intent to sell is a crime. The sale and manufacture of illegal drugs is a crime. Any person who uses illegal drugs is engaging in an illegal act. During the fiscal year ending September 1987, nearly 25% of all people or corporations referred to U.S. prosecuters were suspected of drug law violations. Of these suspects, 87% were suspected of distributing or illegally manufacturing drugs, 9% were suspected of importing drugs, and 4% were suspected of simple possession.[17]

Drug-Related Crime

Specific drug-law violations are not the only crimes committed because of illegal drugs: Murder, extortion, and assault are among the many crimes that stem from the big business of illicit drugs. Experts are interested in two questions: What percentage of crimes is committed because the offender is on drugs and what percentage reflects the offenders' involvement with the drug trade?

One population found to have a higher rate of drug use than the general population is the group known as arrestees, those people who have been arrested for a crime. The National Institute for Justice's 1989 Drug Use Forecasting (DUF) survey concludes that this population shows current drug use to be 10 times that of those polled for NIDA surveys.[18]

Using results from both urinalysis and interviews of over 2,500 arrestees from 16 major cities, the DUF found these results: Between 56% and 84% of male arrestees surveyed tested positive for drugs and between 58% and 88% of females also tested positive. In all but two cities, cocaine, including crack, was the drug most likely to be found. In San Diego and Phoenix, cocaine and marijuana were found in the same quantities. The study limited the number of arrestees who had been charged with drug violations; from that population group, however, between 79% and 93% tested positive for drugs.

Two disturbing trends in the arrestee group were seen: The significant presence of PCP in Washington, D.C. and of amphetamines on the West Coast. In Washington, D.C., 17% of adult arrestees tested positive for PCP, and though this represents a decline from 1987's high rate of 33%, it indicates a trend that is disturbing to officials.

Ice, a cheap, smokable form of methamphetamine, initially reported in Hawaii, remains almost completely a West Coast phenomenon. In San Diego, 34% of males and 33% of females tested positive for amphetamines, compared to 0% in Washington and New York.

The question of whether the offender was under the influence of drugs at the time of the offense is addressed in two surveys. The first is a self-reporting survey of prison inmates and their drug use, and another is the result of victim perception surveys, questionnaires that take into account the victim's perception of their assailant.

In its survey of state prisoners, jail inmates, and youths in long-term custody, the Bureau of Justice Statistics reports that one-third of the state prisoners, one-quarter of convicted jail inmates, and two-fifths of youths in long-term facilities reported that they were under the influence of an illegal drug when they committed the crime for which they were incarcerated. Those with the highest rate of drug use during the offense were those arrested for drug offenses and burglary.[19]

According to the victim perception study of violent offenders from the National Crime Survey conducted in 1988, victims believed their assailants were under the influence of drugs or alcohol in about 36% of violent crimes; victims of rape and assault were more likely than robbery victims to report this observation. In 43% of violent crimes, the victims, especially of robbery, were not able to determine if the assailant was under the influence of drugs or alcohol.[20]

Several studies funded by the NIDA and the National Institute of Justice attempt to reveal the extent to which crime is committed by drug users. Interviews of over 3,000 narcotic (heroin or methadone) and non-narcotic (cocaine, alcohol, marijuana, and sedative) drug users were conducted in Miami, New York City, San Antonio, Dayton, Ohio and Wilmington, Delaware from 1977 to 1985. Researchers believe that, contrary to what one might expect, this group did not seem to either exaggerate or cover up the details of criminal activity. Most often, the group tells the truth "to the best of their ability"; their ability, depending upon the extent of drug use, is sometimes flawed.

These studies uphold the theory that heroin users may be committing upwards of 50 million crimes a year in America and that cocaine and other users are committing almost as many offenses.[21] For example, one group of 573 heroin users from Miami appear to have committed a startling 215,105 offenses in the 12-month period prior to the interviews. Drug violations accounted for about 38%, or 82,000 offenses, and other "victimless" crimes such as prostitution, gambling, and alcohol offenses accounted for 22% of the offenses. Nevertheless, this group of 573 persons were responsible for:

6,000 robberies
6,700 burglaries
900 stolen vehicles
25,000 shoplifting violations
46,000 incidents of larceny and fraud

The number of arrests was incredibly low—of over 215,000 crimes, only 609 resulted in arrest. This equals .3 of 1% or one arrest for every 353 crimes. The group also reported the following incidents for which no arrests were made: 17 cases of arson, 240 of extortion, and 795 of loan-sharking.

The 429 members of the non-narcotic drug group revealed similar criminal activity, though the volume and seriousness of offenses was somewhat less. This group claimed that it had committed about 137,076 crimes or 320 crimes per person in the one-year period. Their arrests equaled about .5%. Two-thirds of the offenses for this group were incidents of shoplifting and drug sales. In general, although both groups were responsible for an inordinate amount of crime, the narcotics drug user commits more crimes, a more diverse number of crimes, and more serious crimes.

Which comes first: drug use or criminal behavior? That question is not easily answered, but the conclusion of this study is that for the non-narcotic user, drugs and crime began at about the same time. For the heroin user, although some type of drug use preceded criminal behavior, heroin use began after criminal behavior had begun. Other studies support the theory that drug use usually begins or coincides with criminal activity, not the other way around. Drugs and crime are intertwined as parts of an underground subculture.

The conclusion of the Miami study was that "the amount of crime drug users committed was far greater than anyone had heretofore imagined, that drug-related crime could at times be exceedingly violent, and that the criminality of heroin and cocaine users was far beyond the control of law enforcement."[22]

Without such offender cooperation, deciding if a crime is drug-related is tricky: Drugs found on the victim or assailant does not necessarily mean the crime was drug-related. When police investigate a crime, they attempt to determine a motive for the offense; a crime is classified as motive known or motive unknown. What kind of circumstances would lead to the conclusion that a crime was drug-related?

The Office of Criminal Justices Plans and Analysis report entitled "Homicide in the District of Columbia" offers some examples of a drug-related homicide: "a person commits murder while under the influence of drugs, a person selling drugs on consignment is killed because he does not pay his supplier, a drug dealer is killed because he tries to short-change his supplier, an argument between a drug dealer and an unsatisfied customer results in murder, drug groups kill outsiders who try to take over the drug market in their territory, or a drug addict attempting to get money to support his drug habit kills someone in the process of a robbery or burglary."[23]

Addressing the relationship between drugs and the high rate of homicide in our cities, the report goes on to state that "Violence is an inherent part of the drug subculture. Homicide is merely a method used to resolve problems that interrupt the flow of business. Homicide is used to create a sense of fear of reprisal, to keep people in line and show who is in control."

Police in Washington, D.C., which had the highest rate of homicides in the country in both 1988 and 1989, estimate that 60% of all homicides in that city were drug-related in both years. When the motive was known to police, the percentage climbed to 80%.

Drugs and the Future of Our Cities

The devastating effects of drug use and the drug trade can be seen clearly on the streets of our cities. Many neighborhoods are now under the control of the drug dealers.

The sale of drugs is out in the open: The use of public housing or abandoned buildings for drug use and sale is common and violence in the streets is all too frequent. The majority of those who live in these communities are not active participants, but their lives are controlled by the violence and intimidation of the drug culture. When to leave the house, what route to take to school, and when or if to stand by the window are the daily, life-or-death decisions the people of these neighborhoods must make.

With fewer options than others, these citizens feel that they are being held hostage by the drug dealers. Many children are not able to leave their homes alone or allowed to play in their yards for fear of being injured or killed. Just walking to and from school is often a dangerous journey. Whole sections of our cities are war zones and innocent people are becoming fatalities in this war.

President Nixon declared war on heroin in 1971; President Reagan declared war on cocaine in the 1980s; and President Bush states that there is an all-out war on drugs today. How has the United States responded to the current and growing drug abuse and drug-related crime problems? The Bush administration has centered its anti-drug policies around crop eradication and law enforcement, including interdiction.

Crop eradication is not a popular method in foreign countries because it alienates those who live there and forces the farmer, the lowest on the ladder, into destitution. The economy of the Andean area has become dependent upon the cultivation and production of cocaine and the power of the major drug cartels is very strong.

Still, the United States must bear some responsibility for finding solutions since the tremendous increase in coca production in Peru and Bolivia is due in large part to the demands of the United States. While every effort should be made to punish those involved in the illegal activities of drugs, including drug kingpins and banks that launder drug money, the economic effects of both coca and opium production cannot be overlooked. Are there ways for the United States to help South American farmers find substitutes for these lucrative crops, perhaps by subsidizing other crops to replace them?

To date, interdiction has focused on stopping drugs from entering the United States rather than on keeping them from exiting the country of origin. It is estimated that we are intercepting no more than 10% of the drugs being imported into the United States. If law enforcement is to succeed, many experts feel that more cooperation between the governments and police departments of foreign countries is necessary.

In the 1990 drug summit in Cartagena, Colombia, President Bush met with the leaders of Peru, Bolivia, and Colombia to discuss a plan of cooperative action to stop the supply of drugs that are coming into the United States. In turn, Colombia's President Virgilio Barco insisted that the United States do more to stop the flow of assault guns from the United States that arm the drug cartels in his country.

Drug use in America is constantly changing—drugs come in and go out of style rather quickly: Marijuana and hallucinogens in the 1960s, PCP in the '70s, powder cocaine in the early '80s, crack cocaine in the late '80s, and heroin, which seems never to go out of style. There are already indications that new and perhaps more dangerous drugs are on the way to the streets of America. *Basuco*, the cheap coca paste currently found on the streets of Colombia, has already hit the city streets of the United States; *epadu* is a coca-like alkaloid from a Colombian tree that is less powerful than cocaine, but also less than half the price. And black tar heroin, produced from Mexican poppies, is a cheaper, but more pure, form of the drug. These or other manufactured drugs may soon become the drugs of choice on the streets. Finding a way to address and reduce the demand for all drugs, including nicotine and alcohol, is of major importance if we are to begin to win the war on drugs here at home. Massive drug treatment and drug education and the reduction of social and economic conditions that give rise to drug use should be part of any drug enforcement plan.

While drug abuse is certainly not limited to any particular economic or ethnic group in the United States, it appears to be declining in the general population while remaining most prevalent in those inner city neighborhoods that offer the least in terms of economic and social opportunities. Gangs of young people are running the drugs in many urban neighborhoods and many more are becoming victims of both drug abuse and the violent drug trade. While juvenile delinquency is not new, most experts believe that the drug trade, in combination with serious economic and social conditions, has contributed to the increase in both juvenile crime and violence.

Notes

1. Malthea Falco, "The Big Business of Illicit Drugs," *Drugs and American Society*. Edited by Robert Emmet Long (New York: The H.W. Wilson Company, 1986), pg. 9.
2. Chris-Ellyn Johanson, *The Encyclopedia of Psychoactive Drugs: Cocaine—The New Epidemic* (New York: Chelsea House Publishers, 1986), pg. 9.
3. Elizabeth Erhlich, "Some Winning Maneuvers in the War on Drugs," *Business Week*, November 27, 1989, pg. 126–130.
4. Gerald Posner, *Warlords of Crime: Chinese Secret Societies: The New Mafia* (New York: Penguin Books, 1988), pg. 20.
5. Chris-Ellyn Johanson, pg. 8.
6. Larry Martz, "A Dirty Drug Secret," *Newsweek*, February 19, 1990, pg. 74.
7. Posner, pg. 21.

8. James A. Inciari, *The War on Drugs: Heroin, Cocaine, Crime and Public Policy* (Palo Alto, CA: Mayfield Publishing Company, 1986), pg. 2.
9. Gordon Wifkin, "The Return of a Deadly Drug Called Horse," *U.S. News and World Report*, August 14, pg. 31.
10. Posner, pg. 261.
11. Gordon Wifkin, pg. 31.
12. Ibid.
13. Susanna McBee, *Drugs and American Society*. "Flood of Drugs—A Losing Battle." Edited by Robert Emmet Long (New York: The H.W. Wilson Company, 1986), pg. 19.
14. Inciardi, pg. 20.
15. John S. Long, *Drugs and American Society*, "Marijuana: A U.S. Farm Crop That's Booming" Edited by Robert Emmet Long (New York: The H.W. Wilson Company, 1986), pg. 104.
16. Ibid., pg. 108.
17. U.S. Department of Justice, Drugs and Crime Facts, 1989, Bureau of Justice Statistics, NCJ-121022, January 1990, pg. 9.
18. U.S. Department of Justice, *Drug Use Forecasting*, National Institute of Justice, April to June 1989, pg. 1.
19. Op. cit., pg. 5.
20. Ibid., pg. 4.
21. Inciardi, pg. 140.
22. Ibid, pg. 119.
23. Office of Criminal Justice Plans and Analysis, *Homicide in the District of Columbia*, 1989, pg. 25.

Juveniles and Crime

It is estimated that over a million children under the age of 18 are seen in some capacity in the juvenile justice system. Although the number of juveniles in the population is decreasing, the number in state custody has actually increased by 10% since 1984. Who are these children? Where did they come from and why are they now held in state facilities under order from the court?

According to the Bureau of Justice Statistics, there were nearly 54,000 juveniles in state-run facilities in February of 1987.[1] Of these, 94% were there for offenses that would be considered criminal if committed by adults, 5% for status offenses, such as running away, and 1% because they had been abused or neglected. The number of juveniles held for alcohol or drug violations has risen by 50% in the last five years. Over half of the juveniles in custody are minorities and the majority of juveniles brought to court for either criminal or status offenses are from lower economic groups.

Juvenile crime has long been a part of American history, but it was during the 1950s that the problem first reached a crisis point. In 1959, sociologist Virginia Held wrote that "juvenile delinquency, particularly in the United States, has come to be considered one of the most urgent social problems of the day, and the epidemic of arrogance and crime seems to be spreading so fast it obliterates the best efforts society can make to control it—or even understand it."[2]

Indeed, during the 1950s the courts and social scientists identified a growing population of juveniles who were committing serious crimes. These were not the kids who skipped school occasionally or who talked back to their mother or stole from the corner fruit stand. These young people looked and acted more threatening; they wore leather jackets, carried switchblades, and belonged to gangs defined by neighborhoods or ethnic ties. Immortalized in movies like *The Wild One, The Blackboard Jungle, Rebel Without a Cause, West Side Story*, and others, these young men and women were the forerunners of the youth gangs so prominent today. Although they terrorized their communities, as do troubled teenagers today, there are many differences between these two groups both in the volume and the types of crime they committed.

In a chilling article entitled "When did our children become killers?," Claude Brown, noted author of *Manchild in the Promised Land*, describes some of the differences he sees between the delinquent of earlier years and today: "In the New York City teen-age gang fights of the 1940s and '50s we used homemade guns, zip guns and knives. On the exceptional occasions when a zip gun actually fired and accidentally wounded someone who happened to be in the unintended line of fire, the shooter was equally as surprised as the victim . . . In the early 1970s it became fashionable among young criminals to kill mugging victims."[3]

Is it true that our young people are more violent and are committing more crimes today or are we hearing more about it through the media?

One way to measure the amount of crime at any given time is to look at the national arrest volume. The Uniform Crime Index shows an increase of 9% in arrests of juveniles for violent crimes and an increase of nearly 5% for property crimes from

1984. Furthermore, in 1988, persons under 18 accounted for 28% of arrests for all Index Crimes.

The largest increase for the five-year period was in the number of arrests for homicide: 1,765 juveniles (under 18) were arrested for the crime of murder, an increase of over 50% from 1984. Arrests for aggravated assault rose nearly 27% and the number of juveniles arrested for drug-law violation rose by about 10%. Arrests of juveniles from city populations over 250,000 accounted for the vast majority of the total number of children arrested.

Youth Gangs

One of the most pressing issues in criminology today is the prevalence of a new brand of youth gang. The United States, as well as several other countries including Canada and the Soviet Union, have seen an increase in the number of gangs in both large and mid-size cities. In the United States, tightly organized gangs, particularly from the Los Angeles area, have expanded their territory and can be found as far east as New York and as far north as Toronto.[4]

While many of the core leaders of such organized gangs as the Crips and Bloods in Los Angeles and Jamaican posses in Boston may be young adults, these and other gangs often recruit those members of the community most vulnerable: children. The average age of a gang member is getting younger; Robert Martin, director of the Chicago Intervention Network, claimed that, while in 1984 the average age of a gang member was 15 years old, in 1987 the average had dropped to 13.5 years old.[5]

While gangs are not a new phenomenon, law enforcement officials believe that the illegal drug trade has changed the nature of them dramatically. For one thing, the amount of money involved in the drug trade is very tempting to a young person, particularly one who feels his or her options are limited. One of the jobs for which juveniles are often recruited is clocking, a term which may come from the standard gold chain worn by dealers that resembles a miniature clock. A lucrative job for an 11- or 12-year old, clocking involves standing on the corner and handing off small amounts of drugs to users. Younger juveniles, sometimes as young as nine or 10, work for gangs as lookouts for police.

The level of gang activity seems to be highest in those areas of our cities where economic and social conditions make children more vulnerable to the temptations of gang life. Juveniles are often courted by gang leaders, befriended in times of need, and made an accepted part of their community. This may be particularly attractive to the child who feels he has little in his life that gives him such hope and acceptance. Typically, the child who is most vulnerable is from an unstable family, has difficulty in school, a poor self-image, and negative role models. Sherwood Jullian, deputy police chief in Phoenix, Arizona, states that gangs usually "breed in an environment where basic institutions, the family, schools, churches, and community organizations are not as strong as we'd like them to be."[6]

Lewis Yablonski, a sociologist, conducted a four-year study of gang violence and found that a gang's core members had severe emotional problems. By forming a group, they seek to "give legitimacy to their violent behavior and avoid being considered insane as might happen if they acted alone." Similar research in Glasgow, Scotland found that gang members are "haunted by a morbid fear that they might be mentally ill."[7]

Officials claim that there were 387 gang-related deaths in Los Angeles in 1987; gang-related violence rose 88% across the nation that same year. Competition over territory and ethnic hatreds can combine to make a wrong look, a wrong clothing color, or an angry word cause for violence and even murder.

Even apart from gangs organized according to territory or ethnic backgrounds, there are also youths who behave in abnormally violent and aggressive ways when they find themselves in groups, such as the 14- and 15-year olds who allegedly attacked, raped, and brutally beat a woman jogger in Central Park in 1987. The children charged in the attack apparently were not part of any organized gang, but police claim the youths rampaged through New York together on what the press described as a "wilding" spree. One of those arrested allegedly stated: "It was fun."

Why Do Children Commit Crime?

Adolescence is an age when the child begins the long road to self-discovery and identity. Most children at this age begin to rebel against the rules and regulations of their parents, teachers, and authority in general. It is a turbulent time, filled with confusion and doubt as well as a great deal of bravado. Adolescents, because they tend to be risk takers, are often dangerous to themselves and to others. Most teenagers, however, find safe ways to express these feelings and are protected from the dangers they seek by their families and communities. Although many may commit minor offenses, most enter adulthood with little or no contact with law enforcement agencies.

Teenagers from affluent suburbs and families have many options not available to those from the inner city: Their families can afford private placements for them if their behavior is a problem to the community, the police are more apt to find alternatives to arrest, such as calling the parents or scaring them with a stern lecture. It is a fact that there is less crime in suburban and rural areas, so the juvenile offenders in these areas are less likely to be observed by police. By contrast, inner city adolescents, particularly black and Hispanic youths, are more apt to be suspected of wrongdoing, even when they are not committing offenses unusual for this rebellious age.

There are others, however, who commit offenses that are deemed criminal regardless of what area one lives in or what social class one belongs to. According to the Uniform Crime Report, more than 1,700 homicides, 4,000 rapes, 38,000 assaults, and 24,000 robberies were committed by children under the age of 18 in 1988. In two recent books, *The Child Savers* and *At a Tender Age*, the authors each spent a year observing juvenile court proceedings in New York City. The crimes committed by the youths that were studied ranged from homicide to robbery. What was particularly striking to these two observers was the number of juveniles—often acting in groups—who committed terrible acts of violence yet expressed little or no remorse about their actions. These are juveniles who rape, beat, and set afire homeless women; who are able to obtain and use guns at the age of 13; and for whom there is literally no one willing to take responsibility. How is it that these children behave in ways that are so different from the majority of kids their age?

There are often social causes for the violent behavior of juveniles, many of them directly related to the deteriorating conditions of our inner cities: Poor education, few job opportunities, poor housing, and unstable families are some of the conditions that can cause the frustration and impulsiveness that leads to violence.[8] These conditions in turn can cause feelings of low self-esteem and self-hatred. Empathy, responsibility, and remorse or feelings of guilt are often characteristics lacking in violent juveniles.

Many experts believe that these young people were not born with these deficiencies, but acquired or learned them as a result of early life experiences. They are frequently from violent, assaultive homes in which parents physically strike one another as well as their children.[9] Other factors such as alcohol and drug abuse also affect behavior, and head injuries that cause neurological damage may well lead to impulsive behavior.

Though they represent a small minority, the number of juveniles who commit violent crimes is very disturbing, both to the society at large as well as to the communities in which they live.

They stand apart from the misguided or troubled child who commits minor offenses and, with maturity or intervention of some kind, gains control over impulsive or criminal behavior. In addition, their victims are often other juveniles. Violence accounts for more than 75% of all deaths among 15- to 24-year olds. Jeanne Taylor, executive director of the Roxbury Comprehensive Community Health Center in Boston, calls these children—both perpetrators and victims—"children of war . . . they've got to be rescued."[10]

The amount of violence to which many children are exposed every day is often astounding. In Baltimore, Maryland, researchers found that 24% of teenagers interviewed at a local clinic had witnessed at least one murder, well over 70% said they personally knew someone that had been killed, and all had witnessed an average of five crimes each.[11] This level of violence is unprecedented and the long-term effects may not be known for another generation.

History of Juvenile Justice

While the number of juveniles who commit serious crime is disturbing, it still remains a very small percentage of the hundreds of thousands of children who find themselves in the juvenile justice system and an even smaller percentage of the total population of juveniles.

Our justice system has always processed juvenile offenders differently than it does adults because we do not consider minors responsible for their actions. Juveniles are protected from harm in a variety of ways. For example, child abuse and neglect laws protect them from physical and psychological injury and child labor laws protect them from unfair or forced labor. Juveniles also face many restrictions, most of which are also seen by the adults as forms of protections: They may not drive or buy cigarettes until age 16 in most states, and they may not buy alcohol until 18 or 21.

Behavior that is seen as unacceptable for a child is also regulated for juveniles by custom and enforced by law; many of these laws and regulations have been the cause of controversy as well as reform within the juvenile justice system. Disobedience, running away, and truancy are behaviors that are unacceptable only for minors.

In Roman law, a father had supreme authority over his children. *Potestas* was the term used to describe the power of the father to "sell, lease, enslave, marry, divorce, or put to death" his children.[12] In the Old Testament, in addition to the Fifth Commandment, which states, "Thou shalt honor and obey your parents," the Book of Dueteronomy (21:18–21) states that a child found guilty of being disloyal and defiant to his or her parents can be stoned to death by the elders of the community.

In the Massachusetts Bay Colony, the Puritans adopted this law, though no cases appear to have been prosecuted. Disobedience of parental authority in our early history was thought to have been as much the fault of the parents as the child; community members in Massachusetts Bay Colony were encouraged to report those parents who did not supervise their children properly. Children were often placed with those families that the community felt would offer the proper spiritual and moral upbringing.

The young people in colonial days were seen as important members of the labor force. At the age of 12, and sometimes before, children worked, as either apprentices or indentured servants. Common offenses for children included running away, swearing, fighting, and disobedience. Capital punishment, though used against children in England during the 17th century, was not common in the colonies. Children were, however, often whipped and sentenced to long terms in prison with adult criminals.

In the early 1800s, more humane treatment of children began with the founding of several social agencies. In 1817, the Society for the Prevention of Pauperism was established in New York, and in 1825, New York's House of Refuge was one of the earliest institutions for children. An alternative to the harsh prisons in existence, the House of Refuge accepted juveniles who had been accused of a crime as well as destitute children for whom, according to authorities, criminal activity was just around the corner. By 1829, more than half of the population was from immigrant families. In 1834, the New York House of Refuge added a separate section for black children.

Until the late 19th century, there was no organized social movement for government involvement in children's behavior. Then, because of industrialization, immigration, and the growth of the cities, large numbers of poor and working-class families found their way to the big cities in America. While the middle class voiced concern about rising poverty and conditions in the inner cities, it was often expressed as criticism of immigrant behavior and family styles.

During the period known as the Progressive Era, from about 1900 to 1917, philosophy regarding children changed. While the Puritans had thought of children as "reflecting the essential sinfulness of man," the more enlightened view held that children were essentially innocent, but also very vulnerable to the evils of society, and in particular, to the criminal behavior of the lower class.

As the middle class became involved in the regulation of the behavior of these children, a more organized movement was under way to bring those who were viewed by the larger society as wayward or unsupervised into the judicial system. Jane Addams helped found the first juvenile court in 1899 in Illinois.

What gave states the right to be essentially another parent to juveniles was the English doctrine called *parens patriae*, which gave the state, through its courts, the authority to act as a super-parent to children in need and to place children in the care and custody of the state. The government could, therefore, determine whether the child would remain at home, be placed in foster care, or be sent to a state-run facility, originally called detention or industrial schools.

The courts' purpose, according to the original philosophy, was not to mete out justice, but to provide for moral rehabilitation. In part because of the reluctance of authorities to brand and stigmatize children as criminals, the juvenile was not to be charged with a specific crime. If children were before the court, they were assumed to be in need of guidance, not punishment. It was not the offense that was in question, it was the child's "status" or life story that the court wanted to hear.

A child could find him- or herself before the courts for offenses considered criminal as well as for activities frequently called "status" offenses. In criminal law, a status offense is one that is based on a condition, i.e., drug addiction or prostitution. In juvenile law, it is based on the condition of being a minor. Status offenses are viewed as wrong only because they are committed by juveniles: Truancy, running away, incorrigibility, vagabondage, association with undesirable persons, presence in undesirable places, undesirable behavior, and disobedience to parents and teachers were common status offenses in the early 1900s.

Informal hearings with a judge for both criminal and status offenses could result in decisions ranging anywhere from probation to commitment until majority (until the age of 18). Status offenders and those who committed crimes were often sent to the same industrial school, but the emphasis was on the rehabilitation of the youthful offender.

The informal setting of the juvenile courts continued until the late 1950s, but the original thinking that led to such hearings began to be reexamined and reformed. It was felt that although the hearings may have been confidential, information regarding a particular child before the court invariably became the knowledge of not only the community, but also various community organizations, including social welfare, schools, and police. Children were, in fact, being branded as delinquent or criminal and, because of others' expectations and the child's own sense of self-esteem, this stigma often increased the child's wayward behavior rather than correcting or preventing it. In addition, the placement of all types of children, no matter the severity of their crimes, in the same facilities was a disastrous policy since relatively innocent children could easily learn more reprehensible behavior while in custody.

A series of reforms that first began in the 1960s have changed the system dramatically. In general, the decade was a period of great upheaval and social change: The rights of minorities, women, and the disenfranchised were of particular concern to those demanding changes in the society. The movement for children's rights was a natural and logical outgrowth of the general movement for extended rights for those in our society without power. Children had been at the mercy of a judicial system that had been virtually unaccountable to anyone on the outside. The decisions it made were informal and confidential and though, for the most part, based on humanitarian concepts, some felt that children needed to be protected from the overwhelming power of the court through the same kinds of legal sanctions that adults were granted in the Constitution.

In 1963, New York clarified its definitions of "delinquents" and "status offenders." Children who commit actual crimes were to be known as delinquents, while those who commit status offenses would be referred to as PINS, Persons in Need of Services, or CHINS, Children in Need of Services. Since that time, most other states in the union have enacted similar laws. Then in 1974 the federal Juvenile Justice and Delinquency Act made federal funding of state and local offender programs contingent on the state's releasing status offenders. No longer could those juveniles accused of status offenses alone be committed to institutions.

In addition to these new state laws, the highest court in the land, the United States Supreme Court, made several decisions that granted to juveniles constitutional rights in court. In 1967, juveniles became entitled to receive notices against them, have legal counsel, to confront and cross-examine witnesses, to have the protection of the Fifth Amendment, to receive a transcript of the court hearing, and have the right to appeal. Finally, in 1970, criminal acts committed by juveniles had to be proven "beyond a reasonable doubt." These rights to due process, previously denied to juveniles, currently provoke controversy and anger from the general public.

There are many who feel that the juvenile court system is too lenient on juvenile offenders, that many are getting away with their crimes when, for instance, their case is dismissed because of lack of evidence or because of other "technicalities." Attorneys who defend juveniles strongly believe that the rights of due process granted to all United States citizens are not loopholes or technicalities. The anger of the public stems from both the number of serious and violent crimes that juveniles commit today and disagreement with the view that juveniles, simply because they are under a certain age, should not be legally responsible for their actions. Other experts, however, see this attitude as potentially harmful to those children who might be salvageable through intervention rather than imprisonment.

When Is a Child an Adult?

Given that there is a population of juveniles who are committing more serious and violent crimes, what should the response be from society? There are those who call for harsher punishment, believing that there are certain juveniles who are beyond hope, who should be held accountable for their actions in an adult court. There are even those critics who call for the death penalty for minors who commit murder.

States vary as to the age of minority; in some states, like New York, the age ends at 16, in others it is 18 or 21. All states have the right, however, to petition the court for permission to try a juvenile accused of a serious crime in adult court. Reasons for such a request vary and the courts look at several factors when considering such a petition: the record of offenses the child has, the seriousness of the current crime, and whether more appropriate facilities are available through the juvenile court. When a juvenile is tried as an adult, he or she is entitled to both the extended rights given to adults, such as a trial by jury, and the full extent of punishments, such as prison sentences and, theoretically, capital punishment.

Instead of depending on an already overburdened court system, there are others who would recommend conducting more prevention programs and funding massive campaigns against social and economic problems which they feel cause juvenile crime: poverty, poor schooling, abuse, and drugs.

The courts are often criticized for not providing proper punishment, not diverting offenders at earlier ages, and not providing appropriate programs for those who are in need. Residential facilities, both restricted and open settings, are often crowded and understaffed and juveniles who are placed in these facilities receive more of an education in crime than they do in rehabilitation.

While there are those who think that the court should be an "all-seeing agency that can hold them within its gaze every step of the way," as a court official remarked, there are others who respond that "there used to be that agency. It was called the family."[13] But once supports such as family, community, church, and schools have failed a child, state and court intervention becomes necessary for the safety of the community and the child.

In many cities, the police departments have formed programs designed to control gang violence and divert juveniles who might be susceptible to gang activities. Prevention and control are methods that might prove more effective than the overburdened judicial system. Part of the difficulty in devising more efficient and effective methods of crime control lies in the inability of criminologists and other experts to discover a universal, underlying cause for crime. How do social and economic conditions affect criminal behavior? Is all such behavior learned or is it possible that genetic factors influence our behavior?

Notes

1. Barbara Allen-Hagen, "Public Juvenile Facilities, 1987: Children in Custody," *Juvenile Justice Bulletin*, October 1988, pg.1.
2. Chrisopher Hibbert, *Roots of Evil: A Social History of Crime and Punishment* (Minerva Press: 1963), pg. 431.
3. Claude Brown, "When Did Our Children Become Killers?" [Wilmington Delaware] *Sunday News Journal*, May 22, 1988, pg. M-1.
4. Kay McKinney, *Juvenile Gangs: Crime and Drug Trafficking*, Juvenile Justice Bulletin, U.S. Department of Justice, NCJ-113767, September 1988, pg. 3.
5. Ibid.
6. Ibid.
7. Ronald H. Baily, *Violence and Aggression*. (New York: Time Life Books, 1976) pg. 129.
8. Alex Poinsett, "Why Are Our Children Killing One Another?," *Ebony*, December 1987, pg. 90.
9. Cathy Lynn Grossman, "The Delinquent Mind: How It Differs from Others," *Miami Herald*, August 3, pg. G-8.
10. Dolores Kong, "City Tries to Stem Youth Violence," *Boston*

Globe, February 25, 1990, pg. 31.

11. Karl Zinsmeister, "Growing Up Scared," *The Atlantic,* June 1990, pg. 50.
12. Sanford H. Kadish, ed., *Encyclopedia of Crime and Justice,* Vol. 3 (New York: The Free Press: A Division of Macmillan, Inc., 1983), pg. 984.
13. Rita Kramer, *At A Tender Age: Violent Youth and Juvenile Justice* (New York: Henry Holt & Company, 1988), pg. 24.

CHAPTER SIX

Causes of Crime

$\mathbf{I}$n 1988 there were over 12,000,000 Crime Index Offenses reported in the United States. They were committed by people of all ethnic groups, all ages, and from all regions of the United States. If there were one proven cause of crime, or just one type of criminal, perhaps it would be possible to eradicate or greatly solve the current crisis. But, as we have seen, there has always been crime of one sort or another in every society. Whenever a society makes rules, there will be a certain number of people who will break them.

Each person who commits a crime does so for his or her own reasons, influenced by a set of life experiences and circumstances unique to that individual, and motivated by desires and needs also unique to his or her life situation. The job of experts concerned with discovering the roots or causes of crime is to find what is common in these sets of circumstances; what, if anything, is so similar that we might find a common solution.

For centuries, the debate concerning the causes of crime has centered on several key questions: Is it possible that criminals are born with inherited factors that cause deviant behavior? Or do those who become criminals learn this behavior, influenced mostly by their environment? In other words, is criminal behavior innate or learned? Or is it a combination of both biology and social conditioning?

Although crime has been present in every civilization throughout history, systematic research into the underlying causes of behavior did not begin in earnest until the late 1800s. Until the turn of the century, researchers focused their studies of crime on the physical or biological attributes of the criminal rather than on the social conditions of the group. One of the first to systematically study crime and offenders was an Italian physician and psychiatrist named Ceseare Lombroso.

Known as the father of criminology, Lombroso studied physical characteristics of convicted prisoners and found that there were many physical features common among criminals. Though he later modified his views, he originally concluded that what was common to the criminals that he studied were their atavistic or primitive features: receding foreheads, prominent chins, and long arms much like our ape-like ancestors. He described these criminals as either insane or "criminaloid" (criminal types), and insisted that their criminal tendencies were the result of these inherited characteristics.

Enrico Ferri, a disciple of Lombroso's, originally examined seasonal factors and their effect on crime statistics, but in 1894 his research linked crime and social class for the first time. He approached the study of criminals from a sociological perspective, that is, by studying the criminal's relationship to society rather than the criminal's individual personality or physical traits. He also recommended that society focus on the prevention rather than the punishment of crime.[1]

By the turn of the century, more and more criminologists were focusing on the relationship between crime and the crowded slum conditions of the cities. William Healy, an American psychiatrist, examined the influence of childhood experience on delinquent behavior in addition to various factors of heredity. A multi-causal approach is commonly used in the never-ending search for the causes of crime. Today, sociologists and criminologists look at many different factors—social, psychological, economic, and biological—when examining the causes of criminal behavior.

The Biology of Criminal Behavior

While most criminologists believe that criminal behavior is learned and not innate, many also feel that there are other factors that influence our ability to make decisions. Although many early theories of criminology have proved false, there remains a great body of research examining how chemistry and biology affect behavior.

More sophisticated than simply measuring skull size or body type and shape, these studies are more apt to conclude that environmental or social conditions *in combination with* inherited characteristics could cause criminal behavior. After all, these researchers say, environment does not affect everyone equally. If social conditions are the same, why are certain children from the same background more prone to delinquency than others?

The majority of crime, especially violent crime, is committed by young men. This fact has led researchers to examine the genetic and bioligical differences between the sexes. Why are boys more aggressive than girls and why are men more violent than women? Do social conditions, that is, the ways in which families and communities treat their boys and girls, encourage more aggressive behavior? Or do genetics hold the key?

In the 1960s, researchers found several genetic abnormalities that they believed pointed to the cause of violent behavior. The "XYY" syndrome was one theory that has since been disregarded. Normal males are born with one male (Y) and one female (X) chromosome; those one in 1,000 males who are born with an extra Y chromosome were found to be disproportionately represented in the prison population. Those who discount this theory believe that men with an extra Y chromosome are also larger and more threatening than others, and are therefore more likely to come to the attention of authorities than others.

This syndrome, though widely publicized at the time because of false rumors that infamous mass murderer Richard Speck had this abnormality, never gained much popularity. It did, however, further the research into biological factors regarding behavior. For instance, after Charles Whitman went on a shooting spree from a Texas tower and subsequently took his own life, an autopsy revealed a massive brain tumor. Could similar brain abnormalities be the cause for other sudden, violent behavior?

Crime and Low Intelligence

Another attempt to find a biological explanation for criminal behavior can be found in studies that may suggest a link between such behavior and low intelligence. Research has shown that some offenders have slightly lower than average I.Q.s— about 91 to 93—while the average for the general population is 100.[2]

How might this lead to crime? The reasoning is this: Low I.Q. leads to school frustration and failure, which leads to anger and resentment, which leads to delinquency.

Proponents of the theory state that low I.Q. scores "signify greater difficulty in grasping the likely consequences of action or in learning the meaning and significance of moral codes." Those who are not good at expressing themselves verbally may resort to other ways, such as threats or force.[3] According to critics who do not trust the accuracy with which I.Q. studies predict academic success, a lower I.Q. does not indicate a lack of potential. School failure can lead to joblessness, increasing the likelihood of criminal involvement.

Evidence to support the theory that the ability to learn is directly related to the potential for criminal behavior comes from studies of juvenile delinquents. Study after study has shown that the majority of young offenders do have learning disorders. How these learning difficulties affect crime statistics is not clear, but some researchers see some correlation between the type of "cloudy and unsophisticated" thinking of these youngsters and their behavior. Many can't read or write, others are grades behind others of their age, and these factors in combination with a lack of understanding of the difference between right and wrong often lead to trouble with the law.[4]

One way to determine whether or not a child has a learning disorder is by studying brain-wave activity. In Denmark, the brain-wave patterns of 129 boys between the ages of 11 and 13 were measured by an electroencephalogram, or EEG. Nine years later, it was discovered that those boys whose EEGs revealed lower than normal frequency alpha waves (8–9 per second as opposed to 10–12 per second) had indeed become deliquents.[5]

Diet and Nutrition

Diet, nutrition, and low blood sugar (hypoglycemia) have also been the subjects of numerous studies concerning behavior. According to researchers quoted in *Science Digest*, the foods we eat provide "many of the substances that influence brain chemistry, and, ultimately, behavior." While nutrition therapies remain controversial, those who advocate different nutrition therapies, such as reducing sugar to control hyperactivity, think that changing one's diet can modify behavior.

Criminologist Stephen Schoenthaler claims he was able to reduce antisocial behavior among young offenders by some 50% by substituting fruit juices and nutritious snacks for the high-sugar foods normally eaten. To determine if this was simply the result of decreasing sugar, he then repeated the experiment, allowing children to eat junk food but increasing their intake of orange juice, which also contains a form of sugar (fructose). Surprisingly, he had the same results: Antisocial behavior had decreased dramatically. It was not sugar, Schoenthaler felt, but the increase in vitamin C, that led to a change in behavior.

Heredity

Another controversial theory about criminal behavior is that some people are born with a predeliction or tendency to be antisocial or deviant in their genetic makeups. James Q. Wilson, noted conservative criminologist, addresses these issues in his book *Crime and Human Nature*, in which he postulates that we can make predictions regarding criminality based on I.Q., body type, and other inherited traits.[6]

Other experts agree that genetic factors, such as temperament and I.Q. can contribute to the likelihood of criminal behavior if other factors are also present. These other factors might include some of the negative environmental influences we've already discussed, such as lack of supervision, abusive parents, and poor role models. These experts contend that just as babies are born with different dispositions, some more fussy or more responsive than others, some are born with tendencies that predispose them to aggressive and criminal behavior.

Such tendencies might include impulsiveness, an inability to form deep emotional attachments, and an appetite for danger or risk-taking. The earlier these tendencies are seen in a child, the higher the risk for crime. In a study at the Washington University School of Medicine, Lee Robins examined the lives of over 500 children first seen at a Missouri child guidance clinic in the 1920s. Thirty years later, more than half of the adults exhibiting antisocial behavior had shown serious symptoms before the age of 11, including impulsiveness, poor school performance, theft, recklessness, and lack of guilt feelings.[7]

A more direct method of studying the possibility of a genetic component to criminality is by studying the behavior of twins. Dozens of such studies from the United States, Japan, West Germany, and the Scandinavian countries, have found that identical twins—those who have exactly the same genetic makeup—are twice as likely to have similar criminal tendencies than fraternal twins.

Studies of identical twins who had been adopted early in life have produced some of the same results. In a study of several thousand boys adopted in Denmark, Sarnoff Mednick found that boys whose biological parents were criminals, while their adoptive parents were not, were more likely to have criminal records than those whose adoptive parents were criminals and biological parents were not.[8] The results remained the same regardless of whether the adoptive parents were aware of the biological family's background or at what age the child was adopted.

Do these studies imply or even mean to imply that criminals are born and that there is little we can do to prevent their future criminal lives? No, say the authors of these and other studies, but they do provide opportunities for prevention. Proponents claim that knowing someone is at risk for delinquency, in much the same way one might be at risk for alcoholism or diabetes, gives us the opportunity for early intervention so that we might prevent such behavior. Critics of these theories, however, worry that making and acting on such predictions could be more harmful than helpful to the young child. Criminality and violence are not viewed as health issues, as heart disease or even alcoholism are, but are behaviors condemned by society.

While these theories involving heredity and biology provide important clues to human behavior, most modern criminologists and sociologists continue to attribute negative social and economic conditions to the increase of crime in America.

The Family and Criminal Behavior

Many researchers look to early childhood experience, particularly within the family, to better understand why people behave the way they do. Early researchers in the field of psychiatry, especially the father of modern psychology, Sigmund Freud, claimed that both unconscious feelings—underlying feelings that we are not aware of but which affect our behavior—and conflicts that remain unresolved for a long time may affect behavior. For example, criminal or deviant behavior could be the result of the person's search for love from an absent father, the desire for punishment for a deed that was never discovered, or an urge to retaliate for real or imagined wrongs.[9]

Modern psychologists look at our early childhood experiences, but now focus more on the overall quality of a child's upbringing than on unconscious or unresolved feelings. The relationships we form with our parents help establish our self-esteem, or, how we feel about ourselves. As we discussed in Chapter Four, it is widely believed that severe abuse and neglect often directly leads to antisocial behavior. One study concluded that at least one out of three delinquents suffer physical abuse at home. Observed behavior is also a factor; by some estimates, 55% of all delinquents have parents who are physically abusive.[10]

The profile of a typical delinquent, drawn from a study by the Juvenile Offender Project, is one whose background included "poverty, shattered families, little supervision, inadequate shelter, school failures, and few positive role models."[11] The delinquent often acts without reason or empathy, has no feelings for his or her victims, and does not connect his or her punishment with any wrongdoing, but only with getting caught.

Much has been written regarding the breakdown of the modern family, particularly the American black family, and its relationship to both poverty and crime. In fact, one author claims that "there is broad agreement—at last—that family disintegration is at the root of many of the social and economic problems that worry us most."12 He does make it clear that there are exceptions to this: Many children from intact families get into trouble and many children from one-parent families excel. Nevertheless, the preponderance of children before the courts as well as adults in prison that are from poor, single-parent families has led experts to look more closely at this relationship.

The statistics show that the number of one-parent families as well as children born out of wedlock has increased dramatically in the last few decades. Though the number of families headed by women has been increasing for the entire population since the 1960s, it has increased the most for black families. It is estimated that more than 42% of white children and 84% of black children born in the 1970s will live for some time with a single mother before they reach the age of 18, a phenomenon unprecedented in this country and, according to some, in the world.

Of course, growing up in a single-parent household is not necessarily a negative experience. But if other negative conditions are also present, then the loss of a male role model and stable family life can deeply effect the life of a child. A probation officer in one of Boston's busiest juvenile courts grew up in a city neighborhood with a single parent but, unlike the children he sees in court, he had strong support from his community. His experience was related in a *Boston Globe* article: "His community managed to convey to him that he was expected to stay out of the courthouse, not in it, and if he did not, 'God wrote that one down.' He said his mother, weary as she was, made him do his homework every night, and his universe was subdivided not by sneaker trees but by parishes. The priests knew him, the merchants knew him, the police in the corner knew him. If the juvenile police officers spotted him on the street— 'even if I wasn't doing anything'—they brought him home."13

Without this kind of social supervision, he might very well have found himself in trouble.

The number of teenage pregnancies has also risen sharply, which may affect crime statistics in the near future. As William Julius Wilson points out, "younger mothers tend to have less education, less work experience, and thus fewer resources."[14] While there are many teenage mothers who have the support of their extended families and community to help with the difficult task of raising a child alone and at such a young age, there are many more who do not have the resources, experience, or necessary support to provide for their children. Others have psychological or drug problems themselves. By conservative estimates 375,000 babies are born to drug-using mothers a year. A new generation of children, born into poverty and drug addiction, is at risk.

Media Violence

Quite apart from biological or familial influences, what all American children have in common is exposure to the most pervasive media in history: television and cinema. What effect does violence in the media have on children? This has been the question of innumerable studies by sociologists and psychologists concerned about the link between increased violence and aggression in our society and the increased amount of violence in television shows and movies.

Although no study has yet to prove scientifically that media violence causes violent behavior, most researchers are convinced that "excessive violence in the media increases the likelihood that at least some of the viewers will behave more violently."[15]

This supposition contends that our early experiences and influences help form our personality; they shape the ways in which we will relate to others and how we resolve conflicts. Habitual, constant, aggressive behavior is most likely learned early in life. Researchers claim that those habits and rules we learn help develop a style of behavior that is very difficult to change after about the age of 10. The amount of television children watch before they are in junior high may directly affect their behavior as young adults.

Excessive television viewing also takes time away from other important developmental tasks such as reading and play. Media violence alone, most researchers would agree, might not cause long-term aggressive behavior, but a steady diet of it in combination with other family and social conditions may indeed be detrimental. The amount of time spent watching, the type of program or movie, the family environment, and the alternatives to the viewed behavior offered by family members and peers are just a few of the influences that could increase or decrease the effects of media violence.

Poverty, Race and Crime

According to the 1987 U.S. Census report, there are presently about 32.5 million people living in poverty in the United States. One out of four children under the age of six lives in poverty.[16] (The government defines the poverty line as $9,890 per year in income for a family of three and $12,675 for a family of four.) In 1986, 69% of our nation's poor were white and about 28% were black.

The effects of poverty, both urban and rural, can be devastating to the hopes and aspirations of those who struggle for a better life. Although we live in an affluent country, poverty is a reality for more than 32 million people in America. The gap between the rich and poor is growing and nowhere is it more visible than in our cities, where 43% of the nation's poor live.[17]

Our cities are no longer the bustling manufacturing centers of the past where skilled and semi-skilled workers of all colors and nationalities could find work and provide a stable home for their families. Since World War II, several factors have led to the current crisis of poverty, unemployment, and crime in our cities. Employment in manufacturing for city populations has decreased more than 10% since 1947, when almost 30% were employed in factories. At the same time, full-time employment in service industries, such as finance, real estate and insurance, has increased from 13% to 28%. Jobs that require less than a high-school diploma decreased from 52% to 21%, while the high-school dropout rate in the cities grew to about 40%, making more and more city dwellers unqualified for the new service-related jobs.[18]

Although there is no consensus regarding the cause of criminal activity, the effects of poverty have often been cited as the underlying reason for certain types of crime. In the early 1900s sociologists began to study delinquents from the growing city slums. From that time until today, the majority of serious crime—those crimes defined as violent and property crime—has been committed in our major cities by young men under the age of 25.

If crime is seen as an individual's response to social conditions, then the conditions of poverty, which include poor schooling, inadequate supervision, poor self-esteem, poor nutrition, and violent behavior, both observed and experienced, often lead to criminal behavior. When these conditions exist for middle-class children, there are often more options available to offset the negative effects of these experiences: tutors for learning disabilities, referrals to preparatory schools instead of juvenile court, and a vast array of educational and recreational outlets for the tremendous amount of free time on the hands of the young.

In some ways, criminal behavior is a matter of opportunity. The temptations and rewards of criminal activity are very different for a corporate executive than those for an unemployed city youth, and their crimes will be very different indeed.

A disproportionate number of blacks and Hispanics live in the poorest sections of our inner cities; minority groups are also vastly overrepresented in crime statistics. One out of four black men ages 20 to 29 is either in prison or on probation or parole. Black families are victimized by crime at nearly double the rate of whites. According to the FBI's Uniform Crime Report, 53% of those arrested for all homicides were black. For city arrests (cities with populations over 250,000), 51% of those arrested for violent crime were black and 34.6% of those arrested for property crime were black.

Concern about the disproportionate number of black offenders and black victims of crime has led to many discussions regarding the relationship between race and crime in the United States. Those who are concerned about the high incidence of crime and violence in black inner-city ghettos study the social and economic conditions of the group as a whole. The present conditions of the cities, where 61% of poor blacks live, have led to both social and economic isolation—miles and miles of our inner cities are without order and stability. And, without legitimate employment opportunities, there is literally nothing to do.

William Julius Williams, a black sociologist, has written poignantly about the millions of inner city black Americans who are left out of the American Dream. He believes that the social and economic isolation of current city life has created an underclass of black Americans who live in dire poverty and hopelessness.

As industry has left the cities, so have the black middle and working classes, leaving behind the most isolated and disadvantaged black families. As the cities crumble, so do the schools, the families, and the social institutions that usually provide stability and normalcy. When working- and middle-class city dwellers live side by side with the poorer dwellers of the city, they provide positive role models for the young and vital information regarding health, work, religion, morals, and family. When these influences are absent and the community becomes more socially isolated, and real job opportunities are drastically reduced, the amount of crime and violence rises.

Though many of the present social factors, such as one-parent black families, are fairly recent trends, the historical or long-term effects of slavery, discrimination, and prejudice are also factors that affect blacks both psychologically and economically.

What have we learned from all the various theories regarding the cause of crime?

First, there is no one cause of crime. Poverty, inadequate supervision, abusive or neglectful parenting, racism, self-hatred and self-destruction, impulsive behavior, and a lack of deep attachments to others are but a few of the underlying social causes of the many crimes committed every day. No single factor alone, neither poverty nor nutrition, abnormal brain waves nor low I.Q., causes a person to become a criminal or completely accounts for the number of different types of criminal behavior. No evidence has ever linked a particular race or ethnic group with criminal tendencies.

If a conclusion can be reached, it might be that causes of criminal behavior appear to be interrelated. It is difficult, for example, to separate the effects of racism from lack of job opportunities, or poor school performance from inadequate nutrition or supervision. The combination of several factors, economic and biological for example, might trigger one person's tendency to become involved in crime.

But whatever the causes or set of causes, the fact is that the United States has a serious crime problem that directly or indirectly affects all of us. Once a crime has been committed, it is the job of the judicial system to determine the guilt or innocence of an individual and the appropriate punishment. Our intricate system of justice must protect the community as well as the individual who is accused of a crime. In the next chapter, we'll explore the way our unique judicial system attempts to balance the needs of the victims with those of the accused to protect our society from crime and violence.

Notes

1. *The Encyclopedia Americana: The International Edition* (Danbury, CT: Grolier, Inc., 1988), Vol. 8, pg. 196.
2. Richard J. Herrnstein and James Q. Wilson, "Are Criminals Made or Born?" *New York Times Magazine*, August 4, 1985, pg. 30.
3. Ibid.
4. Andrea Dorfman, "The Criminal Mind: Body Chemistry and Nutrition," *Science Digest*, Vol. 92, No. 10, pg. 46.
5. Ibid.
6. James Q. Wilson and Richard Herrnstein, *Crime and Human Nature* (New York: Simon and Schuster, 1985).
7. Herrnstein and Wilson, *Are Criminals Made or Born?*, pg. 32.
8. Ibid.
9. Walter Bromberg, *Crime and the Mind: An Outline of Psychiatric Criminology* (Westport, CT: Greenwood Press, 1948), pg. 148.
10. Cathy Lynn Grossman, "The Deliquent Mind: How It Differs from Ours," *Miami Herald*, pg. G-8.
11. Ibid.
12. Karl Zinsmeister, "Growing Up Scared," *The Atlantic*, June 1990, pg. 52.
13. Linda Matchan, "Community's Toubles Resound in Dorchester Court," *Boston Globe*, May 27, 1990, pg. 30.
14. William Julius Wilson, *The Truly Disadvantaged: The Inner City, the Underclass, and Public Policy* (Chicago: University of Chicago Press, 1987), pg. 170.
15. Leonard Berkowitz, "Situational Influences on Reactions to Observed Violence," Journal of Social Issues, Vol. 42, 1988, pg. 108.

16. Sally Jacobs, "In Detroit, A People's War on Drugs, Crime," *Boston Globe*, April 15, 1990, pg. 16.

17. Michael B. Katz, *The Undeserving Poor: From the War on Poverty to the War on Welfare* (New York: Pantheon Books, 1989), pg. 127.

18. Ibid., pg. 127.

CHAPTER SEVEN

The Judicial System

Our judicial system is the third branch of government, separate from, but equal to, the executive and legislative branches. Both state and federal court systems are multilayered and consist of thousands of police, judges, probation and parole officers, court clerks, attorneys, and support personnel. The court system reflects the nature of our federal union; though state courts have authority of their own, they are also bound to the decisions of the federal courts.

On the state level, there are three tiers: The lowest level is the local court, or court of limited and special jurisdiction, which hears civil cases involving small sums of money and misdemeanors; the second tier consists of the trial courts, or courts of general jurisdiction, which hear both civil and serious criminal matters; at the highest level are appellate courts, which hear appeals from the lower courts. The appellate courts do not try cases, but review the facts of the original trial and rule on the legality of the case presented.

The federal courts are organized in the same fashion: There are 97 federal district courts, which try federal cases; 10 courts of appeal; and the United States Supreme Court, which is the court of last resort in our justice system. The Supreme Court rules on only about 10% of the thousands of cases it receives from the lower courts. The Court also interprets federal law and issues relating to the Constitution. Its decisions are far-reaching and affect the whole country.

In a criminal action, the state prosecutes an individual who is accused of a crime; in a civil action, an individual brings an action or a suit against another person for a civil violation. A criminal act often prompts both criminal and civil action. For instance, if John hits Jill and robs her, he can be charged in criminal court with the crimes of assault and robbery, and at the same time be charged in civil court by Jill for punitive damages for both. Criminal procedures aim to punish a wrongdoing and civil procedures aim to recover money and address issues relating to the victim of a crime. The courts and court processes we will discuss in this chapter are primarily criminal in nature, rather than civil.

From Arrest to Sentencing

Once a crime has been committed, the process from the arrest of the suspect to a decision about punishment is a long and complicated one. This process has remained virtually unchanged from the colonial period: investigation, arrest, grand jury indictment, arraignment, trial, admission of evidence, questioning of witnesses, and verdict.

What happens to a person who is arrested? For example, let's assume that John has been suspected by police of committing a robbery in his neighborhood. In order to arrest him, the police must obtain an arrest warrant from a judge and, if they wish to search his apartment, they must also obtain a search warrant. They must convince the judge that they have probable cause to believe that the crime has taken place and that John was the perpetrator, or person who committed it.

After obtaining the proper warrants, the police arrest John, making sure to advise him of his Miranda rights: "You have the right to remain silent. You have the right to have an attorney present . . . Anything you say may be used against you in a court of law. . . ." John is brought to the police station. The police then review the case against John with a prosecutor, who ultimately decides whether the accused can be charged. In this case, the prosecutor is not confident about the case because there is little physical evidence against John, but proceeds because of strong eyewitness accounts.

John is then booked at the police station, that is, the official charges against him are recorded. In his case, John cannot afford an attorney and is not willing to make any statements to the police without an attorney present, as is his right. John is then brought before a judge and hears the official accusations against him and the judge decides if there is probable cause that he committed this crime. The prosecutor is able to convince the judge that there is cause and the case is referred to the grand jury. In the meantime, John has been assigned a court-appointed attorney at no charge to himself.

Next the judge has to decide whether John will go to jail or will be released while waiting for trial. John's Legal Aid attorney has had only one hour to review the case, while the prosecutor has been involved since the arrest. She is able to successfully argue, however, that since this is John's first offense, he should be released on bail. The judge sets reasonable bail and John is released.

A grand jury hears the evidence from the prosecutor and his witnesses. The grand jury deliberates and believes that there is enough evidence against John to proceed with the case. An indictment is issued—John is officially accused of a crime. Barring any complications, the case will go to trial.

After indictment by the grand jury, John returns to court for arraignment. The judge informs John of the charges against him, reminds him of his right to a trial by jury, and asks what his plea will be. The prosecutor has informed the defense attorney that he would be willing to drop the assault charge if John pleads guilty to the robbery, thereby eliminating the need for a trial and reducing the sentence. If he pleads not guilty and is subsequently convicted, John's sentence will be longer than if he accepts the bargain.

John claims that he is innocent and wants to take his chances with a jury. He pleads not guilty. A date is set for trial and, as there is no reason to revoke his bail, John returns home.

During the trial, the 12-member jury listens to the evidence from both the prosecutor and the defense. One of the most important moments in the trial is when the judge reminds the jury that they are to presume that John is innocent. He stresses that the defense does not have to prove John's innocence but, rather, the prosecution must prove that John is guilty beyond a reasonable doubt. John and his attorney decide that John will not take the stand and the jury is made aware that this choice cannot be held against him.

After hearing evidence from both sides, the jury meets in secret and votes to convict John on the assault charge, but not the robbery. At a subsequent sentencing hearing, the prosecutor recommends that John be sentenced to one to three years in prison. The judge reviews the case and recommends probation instead of prison. John will stay out of prison if he meets the requirements of his probation. In his case, he must stay away from the victim of the crime, meet monthly with his probation officer, and not be brought before the court on any subsequent charges. Though John and his attorney would have preferred a verdict of not guilty, they are pleased that there is no prison sentence.

John is a full year and a half older than he was when first arrested for the crime. Not all cases proceed as smoothly through the system as John's, nor are the many legal protections followed so well. For instance, though it is required that an indigent defendent be assigned an attorney immediately fol-lowing arrest, this is not always the case. Many spend days, sometimes weeks, in jail before legal representation is available.

The steps involved in the successful prosecution of crime are many, and each has rules and regulations that must be followed. Each crime prosecuted begins with a police investigation and filing of charges.

The Police

The police are responsible for maintaining order in a community and protecting citizens and property. The police in the United States are organized into approximately 40,000 forces of local, district, county, and state police and the sheriffs and deputies of approximately 35,000 towns and villages.

The police investigate crimes, arrest lawbreakers, patrol the streets, and regulate traffic and highways. Police forces also employ "specialists," often plainclothes officers, who investigate specific crimes such as homicide, drugs, and vice. The day-to-day activities of a police officer, when not crime-specific, include involvement with the community in a variety of ways—speaking to youth groups, administering first aid to accident victims, preventing suicides, even rescuing kittens stuck in trees.

Although each person involved in our justice system is allowed a certain amount of discretion or judgment in deciding when, if, and how to proceed with a criminal matter, it is the police who perhaps have the most difficult choices to make in their day-to-day activities. They often must rely on their own judgment to decide what laws to enforce, when to search or pursue a suspect, and which crimes to investigate.

Police are the most visible form of the judicial system a community has, and how the police conduct themselves in their duties is also public. In recent decades, especially, there has been a great deal of publicity about corruption in police departments and charges of police brutality. The riots in our cities during the '60s as well as several that we experienced during the '80s often were triggered by an incident or perceived incident of police brutality.

The Prosecutor

The role of the prosecutor in the United States judicial system is unique. First, prosecutors are not privately hired by individuals, but are appointed or selected by the state to represent the people—a case is referred to as People vs. Smith. In all but five states, prosecutors are elected officials and are therefore responsible to the citizens they represent. In other states, they are appointed by the mayor or other community officials.

From initial screening through sentencing, prosecutors coordinate the state's case against an individual; they alone decide whether a case will be prosecuted. At each step in the process— arrest, charges filed, a grand jury indictment—the prosecutor reviews the case and decides if the case is strong enough to convict. In addition, the prosecutor makes recommendations regarding pre-trial release, presents evidence and recommendations to grand juries, makes plea-bargaining offers, and is often involved in sentencing decisions. Clearly the amount of power and decision making a prosecutor has, which is not allowed any other branch of government, requires honesty and integrity.

The Defense

In the 19th century, the legal profession was one way for the working class to obtain upward mobility. Many defense attorneys came from the working class, learned the profession through apprenticeships, and served as legal protectors for their communities. Even our early history indicates that the defense lawyers looked carefully at the legality of the criminal process; technicalities, even misspellings, could result in a dismissal.[1]

Every person accused of a crime has the right to be represented by an attorney. The role of a defense attorney is to be an advocate of the accused, protecting his or her legal rights throughout the entire legal process: arrest, lineup, preliminary hearing, trial, sentencing, and appeals. Though defendants have the right to defend themselves, most do not choose this option.

The right to an attorney extends to those who cannot afford a lawyer. Poor clients, who make up about 40% of those charged with a felony, have attorneys appointed by the court in an effort to ensure equality in the courtroom. The quality of representation in court for defendants is vital; they face the loss of liberty if convicted. It would be too simplistic to say that no court-appointed attorneys defend their indigent clients as well as privately secured ones do. It is safe to say, however, that these lawyers, often underpaid, carry case loads much larger than private attorneys. The court proceedings are complicated and, for those in danger of a prison sentence, the stakes are high. Who defends the poor, then, is a very important question.

Rights of the Accused

Do those accused of a crime have too many rights and protections? It may often appear to the public that the accused has more rights than the victim of the crime. There is a general lack of confidence in the system and a sense that guilty people are constantly being freed on technicalities. What are the rights afforded to the accused and why have they been enacted?

Most of these rights are actually guarantees granted by the Bill of Rights in the form of amendments to the Constitution. The originators of the Constitution had lived through the tyranny of English rule; they were often unfairly accused of crimes, their homes and persons searched for no reason, they were abandoned in jail for months before trial and not allowed proper representation. With this in mind, the founding fathers wrote provisions that would guarantee the ordinary citizen every protection against mistreatment from those more powerful. The following amendments limit the power of the government and enhance the power of the individual:

The Fourth Amendment protects citizens from unreasonable search and seizure. The term "unreasonable" is not clearly defined and is often the source of argument and disagreement. Police must have search warrants signed by a judge in order to enter a home. The warrant must specify the area to be searched as well as the articles expected to be found. In most cases, a person may not be taken into custody without an arrest warrant issued by a judge as well.

The Fifth Amendment provides several other guarantees to those accused of a crime. This amendment requires that evidence be presented to a grand jury before an individual can be tried for a crime. This stipulation prevents authorities from bringing charges without cause and allows the public to review the case before it goes to court. The Fifth Amendment also protects the accused from being charged more than once for the same crime. The Fifth Amendment also states that the accused has the right to remain silent and can't be forced to testify against him or herself.

Another stipulation of this important amendment is that no one can be deprived of life, liberty, or property without due process of law. Due process guarantees fairness in the administration of justice; it requires both that the laws enacted are fair and that every citizen in the United States receive a fair trial.

The Sixth Amendment provides the accused with the following protections after arrest: a speedy trial and public trial, a jury selected from the state and district in which the crime took place, a jury that is a "fair cross-section of the community," and legal representation. This amendment also states that no one can be held in jail without being told of the charges and that the accused has the right to confront witnesses.

The Seventh Amendment guarantees the accused a trial by jury if charged with a crime and also grants this right to those sued in civil court.

The Eighth Amendment was written to ensure that a person accused of a crime does not sit in jail until the trial date—bail is employed as a guarantee of return. This also prohibits excessive bail, protects the guilty from unreasonable fines, and cruel or unusual punishment.

The Fourteenth Amendment demands that the laws in every state protect the due process of law.

Many of these rights have been further expanded by subsequent U.S. Supreme Court decisions. During the 1960s, influenced in part by the demands for equality from the Civil Rights movement as well as a growing awareness of discrepancies in police arrest and interrogation procedures, the U.S. Supreme Court, headed by Chief Justice Earl Warren, passed legislation that extended and protected individual rights in state courts. Known as the "due process revolution," the legislation passed by the Warren Court extended the rights of due process for every citizen.

Two of the most important decisions were given in 1963 and 1964. In 1963, the Court ruled in the now famous case, *Miranda* v. *Arizona*, that a defendant must be informed of his or her right to remain silent, have an attorney, and to have the court appoint legal representation if the accused cannot afford it. Those unaware of these rights could easily be forced or tricked into an admission of guilt.

This ruling originally infuriated police, who thought that having to inform every suspect of these rights would impede their ability to make arrests. Now known as reading the Miranda rights, this process has become second nature to most police officers and evidence has shown that this procedure has had little effect on the amount of successful arrests and has become an integral part of the process.[2]

In 1964, the Court ruled in *Escobedo* v. *Illinois* that confessions obtained without the presence of an attorney cannot be used in court. The right to an attorney for those who cannot afford those services was first granted in the Sixth Amendment; this right was extended to federal trials in 1938, further extended to state trials in 1963, and finally in 1972 to any cases that could result in imprisonment.

All of these rights were written and decided upon because the courts believed that the accused needed every protection possible against the more powerful state. They protect all of us, and most particularly those who are more disadvantaged than others. In addition, many of these rulings were a direct response to blatant misuse of power by those in authority, whether by coercion on the part of the police to extract a confession, the use of evidence obtained illegally, or the use of a defendants' ignorance of their rights by the police or prosecutor.

Arrests

Only about one-third of the total crimes committed are discovered and of those, the police themselves uncover only a small percentage—about 3% of violent crimes and 2% of property crimes—through investigation, undercover work, and actual witnessing of crimes. All other crimes that result in arrest are brought to the attention of police by citizens, either by the victim or a member of the victim's household.

Few of the reported crimes that police investigate result in an arrest; in fact, only one in five Index offenses are cleared through arrest.[3] Response time is very important; to actually catch a criminal at the scene of the crime, police only have a matter of seconds before the offender has time to escape.

To make a proper arrest, the officer must either obtain an arrest warrant from the court or show that he or she had probable cause at the time to believe that a crime had been committed and that the suspect committed it. In making the arrest, an officer must make sure that all the proper legal steps are taken or the case may be dismissed. Physical evidence can be a vital part of a criminal case; how an officer obtains this evidence is subject to rules and regulations: For example, evidence obtained through unreasonable search cannot be used in court.

Pretrial Release

Often the judge makes a decision about letting a suspect out of jail before he or she stands trial at what is called the preliminary hearing. Two factors influence the decision to release or detain suspects pending trial: whether they will return for trial and whether they pose a threat to the community. Suspects can be released on their own recognizance (ROR), to the custody of a third party, or they may be required to post bail. Currently, bail is money posted that guarantees the suspect will return for trial, but in the Middle Ages, another person would be used as a guarantee. This person would actually have to take the suspect's place and be tried for the crime if the suspect did not return.

About 85% of all defendants are released pending trial and most return willingly for all court sessions. In fact, according to some studies, only about 4% of those who do not return for trial are regarded as having willfully failed to appear—that is they either have absconded or are brought back by force.[4]

How many of those released are arrested for other crimes before trial? It is estimated that about 16% are re-arrested for other crimes. The longer the time between pre-release and trial, however, the more likely the defendant will be re-arrested.[5]

Plea Bargaining

Defendants may plead guilty, not guilty, not guilty by reason of insanity, and *nolo contendere*. *Nolo contendere* means that the defendant accepts the penalty, but does not admit guilt. Although ultimately the plea entered is the defendant's decision, it is often made after conversations with and recommendations from the defense attorney and the prosecutor. At times, a guilty plea is given in exchange for a less serious charge or in the hope that such a plea from the defendant will be rewarded with a lighter sentence.

Plea bargaining is often seen by the court as an expedient way to speed up the case. In other countries, there is a trial no matter how the defendant pleads, while in the United States, if a defendant pleads guilty to a charge, there is no trial. Why do some consider this a better choice? From the court's point of view, it is because trials are costly and lengthy and an overburdened court system would like to avoid them if possible.

Plea bargaining, according to critics of the practice, actually punishes those who claim their Constitutional right to trial by jury. If defendants exercise this right, they risk a harsher sentence. In a move that appears punitive, prosecutors may use the offender's past record to increase the sentence if the accused is later found guilty by a jury. There are prohibitions against plea bargaining in many states and new sentencing laws also restrict the practice.

The Courtroom

Historically, the laws of a society have been regarded as sacred. The atmosphere or decorum in the modern courtroom, though not as formal as in other countries, nevertheless reflects respect and high regard for the law and those responsible for administering justice. This can be seen quite clearly in the appearance and manner of judges as well as in the deferrence given to them. The long black robes they wear give an impression of formality. When they enter the courtroom, everyone is expected to rise. Judges sit in a chair above all the participants and when they speak, everyone is silent.

The language of the law is also formal, and many times difficult for the ordinary person to understand. The lawyers who argue their cases sometimes appear to be speaking another language, "legal jargon," and while our court system is designed for public participation, this language often excludes those who are not legal experts.

A criminal trial is an "adversary form of proceedings in which two sides confront each other according to elaborate rules."[6]

Both the prosecutor and the defense attorney argue the case, present evidence, question witnesses, and make motions or legal suggestions to the judge in order to win the case. While a prosecutor's main objective is to secure a conviction, the defense attorney's goal is not necessarily to "get the client off," but rather to protect the legal rights of the accused.

In a trial, the participants agree beforehand to several principles: Hearsay evidence (conversations overheard by a third party) shouldn't be admitted; the defendant should be presumed innocent; and the government must prove the case beyond a certain doubt. These principles are not always honored (a prosecutor or defense attorney may attempt to introduce testimony that will be ruled hearsay after the jury hears the testimony), but it is expected that they will be adhered to by all participants, including the jury.

Both sides must conform to the same rules; if all things are equal, neither side has a particular advantage. In fact, the defense does have an advantage in that it does not have to prove the defendant's innocence; it is the prosecutor's responsibility to prove that the defendant is guilty.

The Jury

Juries hear and decide both civil cases—auto-damage suits, for example—and criminal cases. Not everyone is allowed to sit on a jury nor is the entire population represented. Often, for instance, jurists are selected from voter lists, but less than three-fourths of those eligible to vote were registered in 1984.[7]

Jurists are chosen randomly, but can be dismissed for any number of reasons—previous involvement in a similar crime or knowledge of the case before the court, for instance—after being interviewed by either the prosecutor or defense attorney. Those who are employed in certain professions may also be excluded: Lawyers, doctors, police officers, and firefighters are often excluded by statute in many states.

The intent to have the jury represent a cross-section of the population is present, but in reality this may not be the case. Though the court offers some compensation for wages lost during jury duty, many working people cannot afford the difference between this and their regular pay and, in general, such people are under-represented in juries.8 Minorities are also vastly under-represented in juries and the process of accepting or rejecting prospective jurors is often criticized for leading to discrimination against minorities. These practices undermine the intent of the courts to provide a fair trial for all.

Our history, in fact, does not reflect a very good record in jury selection. Blacks were prohibited from serving on juries until 1886 when the Supreme Court ruled that states did not have the right to exclude this group; in the same decision, however, the Court ruled that excluding women from juries was legal. It wasn't until 1940 that the Court reversed this decision.

In every state, a 12-person jury is required for all capital cases; six states allow fewer jurists in felony trials. Juries are made up of ordinary citizens. It is expected that jurists will put aside their personal biases and abide by the instructions and principles of the court, including the presumption of innocence, the various rules of evidence, and the standard of proof beyond a doubt.

After all the evidence has been presented, the judge instructs the jury by explaining relevant issues, summarizing the testimony, commenting on the credibility of witnesses, or discussing other information. If it is a bench trial, then the judge alone reaches a verdict. If a guilty verdict is reached, the judge proceeds with sentencing, many times at a hearing conducted later.

Sentencing

Until very recently, there has been much disparity in sentencing decisions. Sentences given for the same crime can vary from state to state as some states are rather lenient in their punishment of certain crimes, while others mete out very harsh sentences. There is also disparity within states; some courts have the reputation of handing down lighter or harsher sentences.

And there is disparity within courtrooms. While some judges are known as "hanging judges," others are seen as soft on certain types of criminals or crimes. Judges may impose an indeterminate sentence, one that specifies a minimum and maximum sentence length. The prisoner's actual release date, within these limits, is determined by a parole board. Sometimes a judge specifies only the maximum length of sentence. The parole board, again, has the power to determine the date of release within the limit of the maximum sentence.

These sentencing practices, though still followed in most states, have been criticized because of the amount of discretion afforded to the judge and the parole authorities. As a result of these concerns, and in response to public demands for consistency, many states have enacted determinate sentencing laws that require convicted criminals to serve specific lengths of time for specific crimes, with no chance of parole. Mandatory sentences are often given for gun-law or drug violations. Furthermore, sentencing guidelines provide states with formulas for determining the length of sentence based on the defendant's prior record and the seriousness of the offense among other considerations.

In 1984, Congress passed the Sentencing Reform Act, which abolished parole for federal offenders and created the United States Sentencing Commission to formulate guidelines for federal judges. As a result of these guidelines, such as mandatory minimum sentences for drug offenders, the number of convicted defendants sent to jail rose from about 50% in 1987 to almost 75% in 1989. The result has been a huge increase in the prison population.

Serving Time

Except in cases of crimes that carry mandatory sentences, as in a life-imprisonment sentence for first-degree murder or a one-year sentence for gun violations, the prison sentence that is handed down by the judge is longer than the time the offender actually serves. There are several ways a prisoner can be released before the sentence expires.

Mandatory release is based on either automatic or earned "goodtime." In some states, the prisoner will automatically earn up to 15 days goodtime for every month served, other states might credit one day for every two served. Earned goodtime is given to a prisoner for participation in educational or social programs and for good behavior.

Parole is granted by an authorized parole board. After release, the prisoner is supervised by a parole officer and is required to comply with certain restrictions and rules of behavior. The parole board may require that the prisoner live in a particular area, not keep company with other former offenders, and meet regularly with the parole officer. If the rules are violated, the prisoner must return to prison and serve the rest of his or her sentence.

How well does our judicial system protect the rights of the accused as well as the safety of the community? Does race discrimination from arrest to sentencing account for the disproportionate number of minorities in our criminal courts, jails, and on death row? Or does it accurately reflect the results of arrests and convictions for Crime Index and drug-law violations? Does prison work as a deterrent to crime, that is, does the threat of prison prevent people from committing crimes? These are some of the serious issues facing our judicial system today.

Prison is the ultimate destination for most people convicted of a serious crime. Our present prison system is under constant scrutiny and criticism because of the overcrowded and inhumane conditions prisoners often experience. There may be other ways to prevent crime: through education, rehabilitation, treatment and innovative policing techniques. In Chapter Eight, we will discuss some of these alternatives.

Notes

1. Samuel Walker, *Popular Justice: A History of American Criminal Justice*. (New York: Oxford University Press, 1980), pg. 110.
2. Herbert Jacob, *Justice in America: Courts, Lawyers, and the Judicial System*. (Boston: Little, Brown Company, 1984), pg. 110.
3. Marianne W. Zawitz, ed., *Report to the Nation on Crime and Justice: Second Edition*, Bureau of Justice Statistics, NCJ-105506, March 1988, pg. 65.
4. Ibid., pg. 76.
5. Ibid., pg. 77.
6. Ibid., pg. 11.
7. Seymour Wishman, *Anatomy of a Jury*. (New York: Penguin Books, 1986). pg. 29.
8. Herbert Jacob, *Justice in America: Courts, Lawyers, and the Judicial System*. (Boston: Little, Brown Company, 1984), pg. 139.

CHAPTER EIGHT

Fighting Crime in Modern America

What can be done to reduce the amount of crime in the United States? The theories regarding the causes of crime—and therefore the solutions to the crime problem—are often contradictory and none of them alone can account for all the various types of crimes committed. Though there may be common characteristics, there is no one "typical" criminal; the young, violent offender who is also addicted to drugs or alcohol commits a crime for entirely different reasons than the white-collar criminal who nets $1 million from an illegal wire transfer.

The majority of Americans view violent and property crimes as more serious than economic crimes; arrest and sentencing trends reflect that thinking. Public outcry about crime in the streets and demands for public safety have paved the way for national policies that focus on increased enforcement of Crime Index offenses through arrests, stiffer penalties, and increased certainty of incarceration.

In recent years, the efforts of law enforcement, including the judicial system, to control crime has centered on increasing police presence and surveillance techniques in order to increase arrests and convictions. The national response to crime during the Reagan and Bush administrations has concentrated on enforcing stiffer penalties, abolishing probation and parole for federal criminals, and building new prisons to house the increase in prisoners.

In many ways, these policies have been successful. Arrests have increased in the last few years and, as a result of new drug laws and sentencing guidelines, the number of convicted criminals going to prison has almost doubled since 1987.[1] On the other hand, the amount of crime being committed has not decreased.

While most Americans agree that it is necessary to remove the dangerous or repeat offender from the streets, there are many who believe that crime will continue to be a major problem if the nation does not address its underlying causes. Even if we doubled the number of arrests and the number of convicted who serve time, millions of offenses would still be committed each year. In a recent article in *Businessm Week*, author Elizabeth Erhlich suggests that focusing our crime efforts on punishment rather than education and social programs "underscores a failure—of focus and imagination—that plagues federal drug policy in general and threatens to condem the urban poor. Approaches that rebuild lives and communities, and help people take responsibility for themselves, promise to do far more."[2] In this chapter, we will explore some new techniques and suggestions for dealing with crime in America.

Response from Police

A new approach called "problem-solving policing" is changing the way many officers respond to complaints in high-crime areas. The traditional response to crime, particularly since the widespread use of the patrol car, has been "incident-oriented"; that is, police respond to the complaint by taking down the information given and attempting to solve the crime through arrest. Problem-solving or problem-oriented policing encourages the officer to look beyond the particular crime at hand and examine some of the underlying causes of the incident. For example, if a series of crimes are being committed in an unlit alley between buildings, an officer might mobilize the residents or the landlord to install a bright street lamp in the area. The drug dealer or the robber would no longer have a safe place to conduct business.

In 1988, for example, foot patrol officers in Tulsa, Oklahoma were sent into five housing projects that had been plagued by drug-related crime. The police did not merely look for and arrest suspects; they attended resident meetings and attempted to help residents resolve some of the related problems of the community by consulting with drug treatment facilities, schools, and social service agencies. The police in turn were rewarded with increased cooperation from the residents.

By using this strategy, the officer may not be able to solve the most recent complaint, but may increase the chances of preventing the next 20 or 30. If many of the complaints are the result of intolerable living conditions, an officer may be able to force a landlord to fix the heating or broken mailboxes faster than the ordinary tenant could. Though some police departments see these activities as social work and have been reluctant to allow their police to become so involved, others are finding that after using such techniques, crime rates often plummet in formerly high-crime areas.

In neighborhoods plagued by crime, there are often many physical symbols of the collapsing social order. For example, if one broken window remains unfixed in a housing project, then it might be assumed that no one cares about broken windows there. This gives the window breaker permission to break even more windows. This analogy has been used by criminologist James Q. Wilson, who points out that "soon there will be no windows. Likewise, when disorderly behavior—say, rude remarks by loitering youths—is left unchallenged, the signal given is that no one cares."[3] Community-oriented police work is an effort to fix the broken windows by helping residents regain control over their communities. Sometimes it means mobilizing the neighborhood to repaint the graffiti plastered on the street signs, employing homeless people in the stores that file complaints against them, and attending neighborhood meetings. Police in Texas, Virginia, and New York are finding that more direct involvement with the community has led to more successful crime control and increased public confidence.

Why is this a new approach? Traditionally, police have been discouraged from intense community involvement and are frequently transferred from one area to another in order to reduce the possibility of police corruption. It is thought that the officer who has long-term and intimate contact with a certain neighborhood may be more vulnerable to the temptations of corruption. In some areas, patrol officers are not allowed to handle drug cases for just that reason. Ironically, while this policy was enacted to prevent corruption, it often leads to increased distrust of police. When citizens observe patrol cars continuously driving past open-air drug markets, they often assume that the officers are either ignoring this activity or are on the take.

The contact between the police and concerned community residents results in an increase in community respect for the police as well as police respect for the community. Instead of only dealing with the offenders, officers now have the opportunity to work directly with the many concerned and law-abiding citizens.

One type of crime that has benefitted most from increased police-community involvement is domestic violence. Studies from Boston and Minneapolis demonstrate that "fewer than 10% of the addresses from which the police receive calls account for more than 60% of those calls."[4] This means that the same homes are contacting the police over and over again. In half the cases, the police have been called in to the same home five or more times. Most of these cases involve domestic violence. If each officer responds only to the incident and does not take into account the history of the problem, then it is more likely that he or she will merely calm everyone down and leave the scene rather than help the victim and perpetrator to get help. Research shows that arresting the violent spouse or boyfriend rather than merely stabilizing the particular incident dramatically reduces the number of violent incidents.

The cost of separating police from the citizens they serve has been high; the community and the police have been eyeing each other with suspicion for years. The officer who handles only the criminal element in a community is unable to see the community as a whole. Problem-solving techniques are beneficial for both the police and the community.

The Response from Citizens

Many communities have responded to the threat and fear of crime by organizing various self-policing programs or neighborhood crime-watch programs. In our central cities, one out of four families and one in five suburban families is involved in some kind of crime-watch organization.[5] A crime-watch organization can serve many functions in a community. First, it gives back some control of the streets of a neighborhood to its citizens and reduces the feeling of defeat and powerlessness. Second, it can improve police-community relations. Third, it can reduce crime in some areas.

In response to drug-related violence that has taken the lives of so many young people, many parents of hard-hit communities have formed various support and drug- and violence-prevention groups. Called a "people's war on drugs and violence," enraged citizens in Detroit have formed such groups as We the People Reclaiming Our Streets (WE-PRO), which uses aggressive tactics to rid its neighborhoods of violence and drugs.[6] Where young people are being murdered at a rate higher than anywhere else in the country, WE-PRO members march regularly on crack houses, beating on pots and pans, in a brave effort to reclaim their streets. Combined with an increase in police presence, the group's vigilance has driven out many drug dealers; police see a marked difference in the areas where these groups operate.

Another way that communities are attempting to lower crime rates in their neighborhoods is through the educational system. Many leaders see education as the ticket to economic independence and personal fulfillment in America. Marion Wright Edelman, president of The Children's Defense Fund, suggests that eradicating family poverty would "make major inroads in improving the lives of our children and and their educational resources. But we must also raise basic skill levels . . . Schools must identify and provide remedial help and support to children at risk of school failure, of dropping out, and of too-early pregnancy, and who will typically face chronic unemployment and poverty as adults."[7]

Though the leadership for educational success comes from the schools, all members of the community, including the parents, should be active participants in their children's education. If education is to meet the goals of discovery and learning, our schools must also provide a safe and structured environment for all, but especially for those children whose lives are plagued by inconsistency, violence, and fear.

Unfortunately, there are 3,000,000 incidents of attempted or completed crime—including assaults, rape, robbery and theft—every year in our schools.[8] It is estimated that 338,000 children carry a handgun to school, one-third of them do so on a daily basis. Police in New York City must ride the subways with children to ensure their safety as they travel to school, and many schools have installed weapon detectors at their doors. While it is alarming that such precautions are necessary, it is heartening to see that more and more adults are attempting to ensure that our schools are havens for learning, not fear.

Finding New Solutions

The American public is so concerned about the drug problem that, according to a Gallop Poll, 53% of those polled said that they would support an invasion of Colombia by American troops in order to stop the drug flow into the United States.[9] Arrests and incarceration for drug law violations have increased dramatically in the last several years. Efforts to control the supply of cocaine and heroin, however, have been generally ineffective. In 1988, the Rand Corporation predicted that "increased drug interdiction efforts are not likely to greatly affect the availability of cocaine in the United States."[10]

There are a growing number of experts who advocate spending more money on treatment and education rather than on prisons, interdiction, and national summits. The NIDA estimates that 2,000,000 users are in need of drug treatment, while there are only 260,000 available public or private slots. New York's Daytop Village, a residential drug treatment facility, receives over 200 requests a day for admission, and the waiting list for an interview is four to five months long. But 70% of the Administrations' anti-drug budget is for law enforcement, while only 30% is available to fund treatment and education.

In our prisons, where drug abuse and addiction is high, only 11.1% of prisoners were in treatment in 1987. Getting prisoners off drugs while they are incarcerated may lead to lower rates of recidivism. Stay'n Out is one prison drug treatment program that has demonstrated success in keeping its rehabilitated drug users out of prison for longer periods of time: 77% of their graduates were both drug free and remained out of trouble for three years as compared to only 50% of other state parolees.[11] Located in a separate wing of New York State's Arthur Kill prison, the prisoners participate in intensive sessions aimed at resolving some of the key reasons for their drug abuse. Improving self-esteem, learning job and other life skills, building self-awareness, and developing leadership qualities are some of the goals of the workshops. Proponents of the program feel that developing such skills will help offenders adapt to mainstream society and buy into a work ethic.

One controversial solution to illegal drug use is to simply legalize or regulate drugs. This suggestion would require a major shift in philosophy regarding drugs in this country— away from a law enforcement issue and towards a public health one. According to an article in *Financial World*, if drugs were legal, then drug-related crime and violence would be reduced; the government could regulate the quality of the drug and therefore reduce the number of overdoses; addicts could receive medical attention and treatment if requested; and the billions now spent in a futile effort to stem the flow could be spent on prevention and treatment. Further, this policy would not necessarily lead to widespread increase in drug use.[12]

Legalizing drugs is not a new idea, but it remains a very unpopular one. The mood in the country is towards stricter penalties, not lighter ones. The International Narcotics Control Board of the United Nations states that legalization would be "morally indefensible and tantamount to the surrender of the world community to the drug cartel."[13]

The underlying social and economic conditions that may contribute to drug addiction, crime, and violence also need to be examined. These include poverty, inadequate education and the resultant high drop-out rate, social and economic isolation, and family dysfunction.

James Mercy, a sociologist with the federal Centers for Disease Control, states that viewing violence as a national public health issue and finding ways to prevent it rather than merely responding to it are ways to reduce the amount of violence.[14]

Violence prevention programs aim to develop self-esteem, address peer pressure issues, and identify to the agencies involved those youths at high risk for gang membership or drug use. The Boys and Girls clubs of America have developed a program for gang intervention and prevention that is currently being tested in several areas of the United States. The clubs claim a high rate of success in outreach programs with those children already involved with the courts. Of 10,000 kids, only about 7% get in trouble with the police again after the clubs become involved.

In Pottsbory Park, a housing project that has the reputation of being one of the worst in Jacksonville, Florida, the organization opened a clubhouse for the children that offers recreation, sports, arts, and computer skill instruction in an effort to provide alternatives to the streets. Not only are parents involved in the various programs, but also the local police, 130 of whom meet here every week.

Keeping kids off the streets and providing them with alternative role models, and decreasing violent behavior through the development of self-esteem are admirable ideas, but may not be long-term solutions to the many economic and social problems our inner cities are experiencing. Laurence Jones, director of a Boston Boys and Girls Club, states that "Violence prevention workshops and all those kinds of things—that's Band-Aid kind of stuff. The reason why people are mad is because they're not part of the mainstream. They can't get a decent job, they can't get a decent education."[15]

If the poverty in our cities is the result of lack of employment opportunities rather than the residents' lack of desire for jobs, then massive intervention by the government and private sector will be necessary to revitalize our cities and to teach work skills. In an age of budget restraints and the general public's reluctance to fund programs through taxes, this costly solution is not popular. But, in a new book entitled *The Police Mystique*, police officer Anthony V. Bouza criticizes the huge investments made in prisons and surveillance while cutting off or underfunding necessary social and economic programs. He compares the national disregard for the crisis in our cities to the disregard our generals had to our failing policies in Vietnam. "Our urban generals, even as they bail furiously against an overwhelming tide, should be crying out an alarm warning of the holocaust they see clearly coming." Bouza further blames the greed of the "overclass," those privileged members of the society, for disregarding and maintaining poor social conditions.[16]

Michael Katz, author of *The Undeserving Poor*, is not optimistic that these conditions are likely to change: "Because there is little reason to expect the trends in either public social benefits or economics to reverse themselves soon, there is every reason to predict that extensive poverty will disfigure the lives of tens of millions of Americans for the indefinite future and that its emerging features will be etched into the national landscape."[17]

Attacking poverty will not eradicate all crime, but providing full opportunities for all Americans to realize their potential may lead to a reduction in the crimes that result from rage and frustration, hopelessness, and alcohol and drug abuse.

"Crime in the Suites"

Corporate or economic crimes are committed for economic reasons. The prevention of such crimes as insider trading, antitrust and safety violations, and fraud in government is more difficult because these are not always conspicuous crimes. They are often crimes committed by corporations with the knowledge of upper management and are more likely to be covered up than reported. Moreover, the sentences given to those convicted are more likely to be in the form of fines, so the fear of imprisonment is not a deterrent.

The enormous gain for corporate executives who commit such crimes is usually much greater than the penalty they risk if caught and convicted. In this way, the response to white-collar crime from the criminal justice system actually encourages rather than deters the behavior. Although Attorney General Richard Thornburgh promised that cracking down on "crime in the suites" would be a priority of the Justice Department, he withdrew his recent sentencing guidelines for these crimes at the request of President Bush.[18]

To deter potential white-collar criminals, there must be a general sense that the acts are wrong and that they will result in meaningful punishment. Consistency in sentencing, similar to the suggested consistency in sentencing for Index offenses, would be helpful.

There are several possible strategies to deter this type of crime: Through Congressional intervention, prosecutors could recommend real punishment for the crimes, rather than a fine that is insignificant to a large corporation or highly paid executive. An executive who is convicted of a corporate crime could be barred in the future from holding office in publically owned companies in the same way convicted union officials are barred from holding union office.

For those convicted of crimes against the environment, the punishment could involve related community service requirements. If top managers of a corporation were held accountable for the wrongdoing of their employees, then illegal practices might be more likely to be discouraged, rather than overlooked. Fines might take the form of common stock instead of money to be given by the corporation to a victim's compensation fund.

Many times these crimes are committed by high government or corporate officials, leaders on whom the public relies for setting standards of ethical behavior. The crimes reap far more profit for the offender than any of the property Index crimes, yet the punishment is more than likely to be quite lenient. One's position in society should not absolve the offender from punishment; this unfair practice causes further suspicion and distrust of business and of government.

On the other hand, would prison for these offenders be appropriate? Many people now believe that our prison system is not the answer for every offender.

Alternatives to Incarceration

Prisons have become expensive answers to the question of crime: To house a maximum-security prisoner costs approximately $100,000 and a state prisoner about $40,000 a year. The goal of incarceration is to punish and incapacitate the offender; rehabilitation, the original goal of the American penal system, has diminished in importance during the last decade. Although the general trend in sentencing is in the direction of stiffer and more certain prison sentences, overcrowding in prisons and deteriorating conditions have forced the courts to find alternatives to prison. These alternative sentences are usually given to the first offender, the nonviolent criminal, or one who has been convicted of less serious crimes or misdemeanors. Most convicted felons, however, are sentenced to a prison term.

Probation is the most widely used alternative to incarceration. A judge will often "suspend" an offender's prison term in favor of community supervision. A prison sentence may be imposed later by the court if the offender breaks the rules of probation.

An offender also may be sentenced to donate a certain number of hours to community service. For example, a juvenile convicted of vandalism, for whom prison would not serve a positive purpose, could be ordered to paint public buildings. Someone convicted of a crime against an elderly person might be ordered to work in a senior citizen home. For distracted and destructive youths, a sentence that directly involves them in helping the community can offer a rewarding and constructive experience.

Other methods, such as restitution, compensation, and fines are also used in lieu of prison, usually in combination with probation. Each year the courts collect about $1 billion in fines.

A controversial new alternative is the use of electronic monitoring devices, which monitor an offender's whereabouts while he or she remains out of jail and in the community. It is a program used with low-risk probation and parole candidates, pretrial defendants, and work-release graduates. This is not a method that is appropriate for everyone, since the devices are not foolproof. One-third of the 800 offenders monitored in 1987 had been convicted of a major traffic violation such as drunk driving.

As we have seen, no one cause of crime has been discovered or agreed upon. There are no two criminals who are exactly alike, nor are their crimes committed for the same reason. In fact, many criminals commit one offense and never commit another; many others commit a number of crimes and are never caught.

It is, however, a small minority of criminals who account for the vast majority of all crimes. If we were to incapacitate those hard-core or career criminals, the crime rate would probably decrease. New sentencing guidelines may produce those desired results. Age is also an important factor in criminal behavior and many offenders merely outgrow the activity as family and employment become more desirable. Charles Silberman states that "marriage and the family are the most effective correctional institutions we have."[19]

The prevention of crime, both street and white-collar crime, will take commitment and vigilance. The government and private businesses stand in full view of those less privileged. When members of these commit fraud, lie to Congress, produce unsafe products, or engage in criminal practices in order to benefit financially, the rest of the country becomes just a little more cynical about respecting and obeying the law. And when sentencing is consistently harsher for robbery than fraud, the public loses confidence in the judicial system. The National Advisory Commission on Standards and Goals stated in its 1973 report that "as long as official corruption exists, the war against crime will be perceived by many as a war of the powerful against the powerless; 'law and order' will be just a hypocritical rallying cry, and 'equal justice under law' will be an empty phrase."[20]

Citizens cannot allow the violence of the streets to continue to take the lives of young people nor the temptation of drug use or the lucrative drug trade to destroy communities. Yet what alternatives are being offered to our urban citizens? Industry and a stable white and black middle class have all but abandoned our cities, leaving few jobs and fewer positive role models in the poorer communities. A major commitment from government and private industry will be necessary to revitalize the cities and offer the American Dream to all our citizens.

Notes

1. Francesca D. Bowman, "The High—and Rising—Costs of More Prisons," *Boston Globe*, May 6, 1990, pg. A24.
2. Elizabeth Ehrlich, "Some Winning Maneuvers in the War on Drugs," *Business Week*, November 27, 1989, pg. 127.
3. James Q. Wilson and George L. Kelling, "Making Neighborhoods Safe," *The Atlantic*, February 1989, pg. 48.
4. Ibid., pg. 49.
5. Marianne W. Zawitz, ed., *Report to the Nation on Crime and Justice: Second Edition*, Bureau of Justice Statistics, NCJ-105506, March 1988, pg. 30.
6. Sally Jacobs, "A People's War on Drugs, Crime," *Boston*

Globe, April 15, 1990, pg. 30.
7. Marion Wright Edelman, "We Must Convey to the Children That We Believe in Them," *Ebony*, August 1988, pg. 133.
8. Karl Zinsmeister, "Growing Up Scared," *The Atlantic*, June 1990, pg. 51.
9. Ellen Benoit, "Drugs: The Case for Legalization," *Financial World*, October 3, 1989, pg. 33.
10. Ibid.
11. Elizabeth Ehrlich, pg. 122.
12. Op. cit.
13. Test Gest, "The Growing Movement to Legalize Drugs," *U.S. World and News Report*, January 22, 1990, pg. 23.
14. Dolores Kong, "A City Tries to Stem Youth Violence," *Boston Globe*, February 25, 1990, pg. 31.
15. Ibid.
16. Anthony V. Bouza, *The Police Mystique: An Insider's Look at Cops, Crime and the Criminal Justice System* (New York: Plenum Press, 1990), pg. 129.
17. Michael Katz, *The Undeserving Poor: From the War on Poverty to the War on Welfare* (New York: Pantheon Books, 1989), pg. 244.
18. Associated Press, "Thornburgh Talks of Upscale Crime," *Boston Globe*, May 9, 1990, pg. 31.
19. Charles Silberman, *Criminal Violence, Criminal Justice* (New York: Random House, 1978), pg. 67.
20. National Advisory Commission on Criminal Justice Standards and Goals, *Community Crime Prevention* (Washington, D.C.: U.S. Government Printing Office, 1972), pg. 207.

Suggestions for Further Reading

Bouza, Anthony V. *The Police Mystique: An Insider's Look at Cops, Crime, and the Criminal Justice System*. New York: Plenum Press, 1990.

Browning, Frank, and John Gerassi. *The American Way of Crime: From Salem to Watergate*. New York: G.P. Putnam's Sons, 1980.

Brownmiller, Susan. *Against Our Will: Men, Women and Rape*. New York: Simon and Shuster, 1975.

Clark, Ramsey. *Crime in America: Observations on Its Nature, Causes, Prevention and Control*. New York: Simon and Schuster, 1970.

Hibbert, Christopher. *The Roots of Evil: A Social History of Crime and Punishment*. New York: Minerva Press, 1963.

Hofstader, Richard, and Michael Wallace, ed. *Violence: A Documentary History*. New York: Alfred A. Knopf, 1981.

Inciardi, James, A. *The War on Drugs: Heroin, Cocaine, Crime, and Public Policy*. Palo Alto, CA: Mayfield Publishing Company, 1986.

Jacob, Herbert. *Justice in America: Courts, Lawyers, and the Judicial System*. Boston: Little, Brown Company, 1986.

Kadish, Sanford H. *Encyclopedia of Crime and Justice*. 4 vols. New York: The Free Press, A Division of Macmillan, Inc., 1983.

Katz, Michael. *The Undeserving Poor: From the War on Poverty to the War on Welfare*. New York: Pantheon Books, 1989.

Kramer, Rita. *At A Tender Age: Violent Youth and Juvenile Justice*. New York: Henry Holt and Company, 1988.

Long, Robert Emmet, ed. *Drugs in American Society*. New York: The H.W. Wilson Company, 1986.

Mokhiber, Russell. *Corporate Crime and Violence: Big Business Power and the Abuse of the Public Trust*. San Francisco, CA: Sierra Club Books, 1988.

Posner, Gerald L. *Warlords of Crime: Chinese Secret Societies: The New Mafia*. New York: Penguin Books, 1988.

Prescott, Peter S. *The Child Savers: Juvenile Justice Observed*. New York: Alfred A. Knopf, 1981.

Safikis, Carl, ed. *The Encyclopedia of American Crime*. New York: Facts On File, Inc., 1982.

Silberman, Charles. *Criminal Violence, Criminal Justice*. New York: Random House, 1978.

Walker, Samuel. *Popular Justice: A History of American Criminal Justice*. New York: Oxford University Press, 1980.

Wilson, James Q., and Richard J. Herrnstein. *Crime and Human Nature*. New York: Simon and Schuster, 1985.

Wilson, William Julius. *The Truly Disadvantaged: The Inner City, the Underclass, and Public Policy*. Chicago: University of Chicago Press, 1987.

INDEX